Historic Acadia
National Park

The Stories Behind One of America's Great Treasures

Catherine Schmitt

Guilford, Connecticut

An imprint of Rowman & Littlefield

Distributed by NATIONAL BOOK NETWORK

Copyright © 2016 Rowman & Littlefield

British Library Cataloguing in Publication Information Available

Library of Congress Cataloging-in-Publication Data

Names: Schmitt, Catherine, author.
Title: Historic Acadia National Park : the stories behind one of America's great treasures / Catherine Schmitt.
Description: Guilford, Connecticut : Lyons Press, [2016] | "Historic Acadia National Park is a collection of true stories that share different aspects of the park's history, from its glacial origins, to its rising peaks near tourist town Bar Harbor. Many of the tales focus on some of Maine's most famous land formations, the people who first walked these woods, and how Acadia National Park evolved into the national treasure it is today."—Provided by publisher. | Includes bibliographical references and index.
Identifiers: LCCN 2016003867 | ISBN 9781493018130 (pbk. : alk. paper) | ISBN 9781493018147 (ebk.).
Subjects: LCSH: Acadia National Park (Me.)—History.
Classification: LCC F27.M9 S27 2016 | DDC 974.1/45—dc23 LC record available at http://lccn.loc.gov/2016003867

CONTENTS

Acknowledgments

To write about a place as beloved as Acadia is an honor and a gift, and also a challenge. Many, many people contributed to this book.

First I must thank everyone at the National Park Service, many of whom took time out of their busy days to talk to me, walk with me, and review text, including Bruce Connery, Judy Hazen Connery, Heather Cooney, John Kelly, David Manski, Abe Miller-Rushing, Emily Pagan, and Gary Stellpflug. Curator Marie Yarborough, Emma Albee, and Kristin Dillon were incredibly generous with their time and knowledge and provided access to much of the archival material and images that are the core of this book. Thanks, especially, to Rebecca Cole-Will for her support and encouragement.

Pauline Angione, Duane Braun, Aimee Beal Church, Sean Cox, Ronald Epp, Ivan Fernandez, Richard Judd, Joseph Kelley, Jim Levitt, Alice Long, Harold Nelson, Sarah Nelson, Earle Shettleworth, Natalie Springuel, Randy Stakeman, Albert Theberge, Helen Townsend, Ciona Ulbrich, Allen Workman, and Bill Zoellick—thank you for sharing your knowledge and expertise. Sean Todd and Toby Stephenson of College of the Atlantic took me out to Mount Desert Rock for some much-needed perspective. Tim Garrity and Maureen Fournier reviewed the manuscript, helped with sources, and provided motivation.

Others welcomed me into their homes and shared their own memories of Acadia, including Nick Burnett, Ben Emory, Anne Funderburk, Wendy Gamble, Alec Goriansky, Mary Morgan, Jack Russell, Larry Taylor, and Jim Wilson. Special thanks to Paul Fremont-Smith.

Research was conducted at Bangor Public Library, Fogler Library at the University of Maine, Harvard University, Jesup Memorial Library, Massachusetts Historical Society, Mount Desert Island Historical Society, Northeast Harbor Library, Osher Map Library, Seal Harbor Village Improvement Society, Southwest Harbor Library, and the William Otis Sawtelle Collections and Research Center at Acadia National Park Headquarters.

Research on the Champlain Society and science in Acadia was supported by a Fitz Eugene Dixon Fellowship from the Schoodic Institute and a period as writer-in-residence with Acadia National Park. Maine Sea Grant and University of Maine provided additional support.

Some of this material appeared previously in *Friends of Acadia Journal*, *Island Journal*, *Maine Boats, Homes & Harbors*, and *Chebacco*. Thanks to the editors of these publications for helping me tell Acadia's stories.

Thanks to Mike Urban for conceiving of this series and inviting me to be a part of it, to Michael Steere for sending him my way, and the teams at Lyons Press and Rowman & Littlefield.

Thanks to my family and friends for their understanding and support, most of all to Eric Green for believing in me, reading drafts, and keeping me company on research trips, interviews, and hikes that always turned out longer than expected.

Finally, my gratitude for Acadia is as infinite as the place itself: magic and beauty enough for everyone.

Foundations

The Landscape That Became Acadia

*As the waves rise and fall in broken rhythm on the shore, as the tide
flows and ebbs across the littoral belt, so the seas of former times have
risen and fallen in uneven measure on the uneasy land; the rocks have
grown and wasted; the ice of the North has crept down and melted
away;—all shifting back and forth in their cycles of change. Only one
scene lies before us of the many that have floated through the past.*
—WILLIAM MORRIS DAVIS, *AN OUTLINE OF
THE GEOLOGY OF MOUNT DESERT*

ON THE EASTERN SIDES OF MOUNT DESERT ISLAND'S HILLS, THE
beginning of Acadia National Park can be found amid giant blocks of
granite, crag upon mossy crag, some tilted, others vertical as walls, their
faces dripping with ferns and rough with lichen. Cedars grow atop and
in between the rock; birch, beech, white pine, and hemlock grow in shafts
of sunlight.

The sheer, tall cliffs form an even line along the topographic con-
tour at 225 feet in elevation. The rock walls are interrupted in places: A
cave opens up at the base of Cadillac Cliffs; a perfect sphere of rock is
lodged deep within the damp abyss. On Day Mountain, a sudden tower
of granite; angular pieces stacked in a column, separated from the wall
by a good two feet. Below, the forest slopes down to the east. It is hard
to imagine a place that seems so solid has been through eons of upheaval
and transformation.

Magnificent, scenic landscapes define America's national parks. At Acadia the landscape is defined by geology. Rock is everywhere. Samuel de Champlain named the island where the majority of the park is located *Isle des Monts Déserts*, "island of barren mountains," in reference to the bare, sloping bedrock summits.

The mountains and coastal headlands—granite promontories now so definitive at the surface—are part of a long-lost continent formed from molten magma three miles below the surface and exposed by millions of years of erosion, hydrothermal and volcanic eruptions, recrystallization, oceans opening and closing, and collision.

The oldest part of Acadia, Ellsworth Schist, dates to about five hundred million years ago. It pokes through in places, along the northwestern edge of Mount Desert and Thompson Islands, grayish schist with wavy streaks of white quartz. Once the floor of an ancient sea, the marine mud was bent and warped by time and motion, folded with white and gray layers of volcanic ash.

The next oldest rock, the Bar Harbor Formation, consists of tan, gray, and lavender sandstones and siltstones visible along the Bar Harbor waterfront.

Cadillac Mountain granite is the most dominant and distinctive: coarse-grained feldspar, flecked with black hornblende and weathered pink by millennia of rain, snow, and sun. Similar granite occurs in Somesville, where it was quarried in the late 1800s and early 1900s.

Geologists describe a wide "shatter zone" surrounding the Cadillac Mountain area, where an intrusion of magma sent splinters of older rock into younger granite. More magma erupted at the surface and cooled into volcanic bedrock visible at Bass Harbor and Cranberry Isles. Remnants of the magma chamber formed part of Isle au Haut.

All of this activity—tectonic shifts and eruptions of the earth's crust—created the bedrock, a resistant granite core, that became the surface features of the landscape, raw material later shaped by a different force: ice. Over the last two million years, cyclical changes in the earth's orbit, tilt, and spin caused changes in global climate, resulting in long periods of cold temperatures and glacial ice cover, alternating with shorter warm, or interglacial, periods.

The most recent cold phase began around one hundred thousand years ago when the earth began, again, to cool. It cooled so much that one year, when summer came, the winter snow did not melt. The next winter, more snow fell onto the old snowpack and did not melt. Yearly layers of snow compacted into ice, building at the center, pushing ice out to the sides, creating movement, spreading. This is the ice that left the most visible mark upon Acadia.

The east–west bedrock ridge of Mount Desert blocked the advancing edge of the glacier. Ice piled up on the north side of Mount Desert and flowed around to the east and west, filling the low areas. It continued to build, thickening into a layer of moving ice, amassing into a giant sheet covering northeastern North America. At its maximum, the ice sheet extended a thousand miles from its center near Hudson's Bay to Long Island, Cape Cod, and out into the ocean, as far as Georges Bank. Acadia was buried beneath a mile of ice.

Scattered throughout the park are random boulders, some perched precariously on mountains, others hidden by forest. These boulders, called erratics, became frozen in the glacier and were transported far from their origins. Examples are Bubble Rock and the gray granite boulders on Cadillac Mountain that came from Lucerne, twenty miles north.

The advancing ice dragged rocks across the granite, leaving long striations and rows of curved chatter marks, or gouges, along gently sloped ridges. As the glacier moved, some of it melted and refroze in bedrock fractures, loosening chunks of rock later plucked away by more ice, shearing away the south-facing slopes, like the Beehive, into blocky cliffs. Along more coherent bedrock, the glacier smoothed and polished the north sides of the hills into streamlined "whalebacks."

Around twenty-one thousand years ago, the earth wobbled again. The glaciers began to melt, their vertical edges calving icebergs into the adjacent sea as their centers grew thinner over land.

The ice disintegrated from south to north, hundreds of feet per year. Again, Acadia's mountains forced the waning ice to pause. The peaks of Sargent and Cadillac Mountains emerged as nunataks—islands in the ice—16,600 years ago, ridges of rock surrounded by ice and sea. Hundreds of feet of ice still covered the rest of Mount Desert Island, Schoodic, and

The sloping bedrock of Mount Desert, 1909. W. C. ALDEN / US GEOLOGICAL SURVEY

Isle au Haut, and continued to grind the granite as it melted. Beneath and around the ice, glacial meltwater cut channels in the rock, gorges that would eventually dry out but retain their distinctive U shape.

Lobes of ice filled the valleys. Ice acted like a bulldozer, piling up ridges of rock debris along the margins, jumbled piles of cobble and silt. Over the years the ice and meltwater beneath it stacked up gravel and rock into moraines, such as at the south end of Jordan Pond. The rate of melting accelerated as the glacier shrank: from one hundred feet per year to five hundred feet per year.

Today it is common knowledge that glaciers created the landscape of Acadia. Not so two hundred years ago, when Charles T. Jackson, a young Boston physician, conducted the first scientific survey of Maine from 1835 to 1837, at the request of the Maine legislature. Jackson was primarily looking for mineral resources and spent only a brief time on Mount Desert Island. In his *Report on the Geology of the State of Maine*, he explained that gravel deposits, erratic boulders, scratched rock, and eroded valleys were caused by moving water. A lot of water. *A great flood.* The earth, after all, was young, young enough to have been written about *in the beginning*, and so most of what had happened had been witnessed by man and written down. No text said that *ice* had done this work, nor that the whole world had been colder and was still thawing out.

Jackson's theory was diluvian, or Noachian: Noah's flood created the landscape. He concluded from his work there and elsewhere in the state that

> *all the observations that have been made, tend to prove that a current of water has swept over the surface of the globe . . . and that the current swept along with it, the loose masses of stone and gravel and sand, carrying them from the north or northwest toward the south or southeast. Thus was formed the accumulation of rounded masses of stones and gravel and clay, which constitute what is called, by geologists, diluvial soil. It is supposed that this rushing of water over the land, took place during the last grand deluge, accounts of which have been handed down by tradition, and are preserved in the archives of all people. Although it is commonly supposed that the deluge was intended solely for the punishment of the corrupt antediluvians, it is not improbable, that the descendants of Noah reap many advantages from its influence, since the various soils underwent modifications and admixtures, which rendered them better adapted to the wants of man. May not the hand of Benevolence be seen working, even amid the waters of the deluge?*

Jackson's words reflected the intellectual consensus of his era. Like Jackson, other scientists studied the landscape of Acadia. Attracted by the area's striking and obvious geology, they came in search of evidence to support their hypotheses about how life on earth came to be. Naturalists and scientists had been debating the causes of surficial geologic features and questioning the age and formation of the earth, challenging religious beliefs at a time when science was still emerging as an independent discipline.

Franz Graeter's illustration, "Granite Mountains, Mount Desert," Plate XXI in *Atlas of Plates Illustrating the Geology of the State of Maine*, 1837. COURTESY OF SPECIAL COLLECTIONS, RAYMOND H. FOGLER LIBRARY, UNIVERSITY OF MAINE, ORONO, MAINE

Charles Hitchcock and Ezekiel Holmes expanded Jackson's work with a second state geological survey in 1861 and 1862. They, too, tried (with difficulty) to explain Acadia's features in terms of the Great Flood. By then, some geologists had come to acknowledge the role of frozen water, but in the form of floating icebergs.

Hitchcock and Holmes corresponded with John Kimball DeLaski, a local physician with an interest in geology who had been making observations around his Vinalhaven home in Penobscot Bay. DeLaski disregarded floating icebergs as an explanation. A careful observer of the landscape, he concluded that an immense ice sheet had recently covered much of northeastern North America.

After seeing (and writing about) glacial evidence in his backyard, DeLaski went to the mountains on either side of Penobscot Bay to determine how high the glacier might have reached. In a lengthy unpublished manuscript, he described the approach to Acadia. The Mount Desert hills seemed to leap up tall and gigantic from the earth as if awakened at the sound of a trumpet.

The foot-marks of the glacier along this road all assure you that it came from the north. On the road towards Bar Harbor the scratch and polish are everywhere abundant. Standing upon the highest hill of this group and having everywhere seen the tremendous denudation to which it has evidently been subjected, I cannot perceive how it is possible for an intelligent man to attribute this destruction to any other agency than that of a glacier, which once overrode these mountains.

DeLaski's observations at Acadia, which were clearly gathered over extensive and frequent visits, allowed him to calculate that the great ice sheet was at least four thousand feet thick.

In their recent publication of DeLaski's manuscript, Maine geologists Harold Borns and Kirk Maasch wrote it is likely that DeLaski was the "naturalist friend" who played tour guide to Swiss scientist and Harvard zoology professor Louis Agassiz when he traveled to Maine in 1864.

Agassiz had first introduced the idea of an *eiszeit,* an ice age, in Europe in 1837. Not only were existing glaciers much bigger in the past, he proposed, but other areas currently without snow or ice were once covered by glaciers, too. For the next several decades, working with Oxford professor Reverend William Buckland and others, Agassiz assembled from his observations the glacier theory that would earn him credit as a codiscoverer of the last ice age.

Agassiz, too, wrote about crossing the bridge to Mount Desert Island and seeing grooves and scratches. He and DeLaski likely discussed how the scratches always ran in one direction, south to north, ascending all the elevations and descending into all the depressions. Addressing his critics in the *Atlantic Monthly,* Agassiz wrote, "If not openly said, it is whispered, that, after all, this great ice-period is a mere fancy, worthy at best of a place among the tales of the Arabian Nights." The naturalist colleagues visited Great Head and Sand Beach and climbed Cadillac Mountain, noticing all the time polished and grooved surfaces and scratches.

To DeLaski and Agassiz, the signature of ice was obvious. They could see the solid weight of it: "Every natural surface of rock is scored by its writing, and even the tops of the mountains attest, by their rounded and polished summits, that they formed no obstacle to its advance."

Agassiz believed that, like a great flood, ice, too, could be the work of a Creator. He described the ice as "God's great plow."

⁓

Understanding of the complex interactions of climate, land, sea, ice, and water came slowly. Acadia's prominent geology continued to attract renowned scientists, and their accounts provide a glimpse into the history of geologic thought.

Nathaniel Southgate Shaler first visited Acadia in 1860, when he was a student under Agassiz at Harvard. He became a Harvard professor of paleontology and geology and continued to visit the Maine coast, first with the Coast Survey from 1870 to 1872, publishing "Report on the Recent Changes of Level on the Coast of Maine" in 1874. Later, working under the US Geological Survey, he conducted what is considered the first systematic study of Mount Desert's surficial and bedrock geology. By this time, Agassiz, DeLaski, and others had helped Americans see the work of past climate changes on their home ground, and the ice age was no longer a mere whisper. So Shaler wrote, "There can be no question that ice covered the hills to their summits, and that it was deep upon the tops of the highest peaks."

Shaler spent much of his time with the Geological Survey documenting how sea level—the boundary between ocean and land—varied over time.

The fact that the ice sheet was in contact with the sea complicated Maine's deglaciation story. With so much water tied up in ice, the edge of the sea was hundreds of feet lower but got higher as the glacier melted, eroding the southern edge of the ice, which broke apart into icebergs and slush. The ice had gotten heavy as it accumulated (260 quadrillion tons by one estimate), pushing down on the land, allowing the rising Atlantic Ocean to flood into low-lying areas in the glacier's wake. This "DeGeer Sea," named for Swedish geologist Bernard DeGeer, reached its highest

Nathaniel Southgate Shaler, ca. 1894.
WIKIMEDIA COMMONS

extent, or "highstand," fifteen thousand years ago, when Mount Desert was a row of nine islands in the young sea.

No one has any idea how long the highstand lasted, just that it had to be long enough for erosional features to form. Waves crashed against Acadia's mountainsides, fracturing and splitting bedrock along weak spots and fault lines, breaking away fragments and eroding the softer rocks, leaving behind cliffs, caves, chasms, and "sea stacks" of more resistant rock. Valleys were inundated with salt water. In marine lakes and quieter coves, silt settled to the seafloor.

Geologists have a saying, "The present is key to the past." Shaler studied Acadia's shoreline and then went looking for similar features higher up the mountain slopes. At the time no one knew how much the ice had depressed the earth's crust, or how high the sea had been, or how rapidly the land rebounded. Shaler did not know that the present shoreline he knew and studied so carefully had been exposed to waves for much, much longer than the ancient shoreline he sought.

According to modern geologists, most of the rocks on the Maine coast have too many fractures to allow features like sea stacks to form

Illustration of the Day Mountain sea stack or "pulpit rock," from "The Geology of Mount Desert" by N. S. Shaler, in the Eighth Annual Report of the U.S. Geological Survey, 1889.
D.L.W. GILL / US GEOLOGICAL SURVEY

or exist for very long, but the granite of Mount Desert Island is ideal for their formation. Still, other forces could create stone pillars, worn rock faces, and eroded cliffs. The only features unique to sea erosion are smooth cobble beaches, like the one found amid the forest in the cleft of Day Mountain, or the perfectly rounded stones lodged within a cave at Cadillac Cliffs. Seduced by the myriad expressions of time in Acadia's rocks, Shaler mistakenly claimed a shoreline as high as 1,300 feet.

Shaler used notes and maps sketched by his Harvard colleague William Morris Davis. Davis had been studying the geology of Mount Desert since 1880, when he joined some of his students at their camp in Northeast Harbor. The students had spent a productive summer surveying the natural history of the island under the leadership of Charles Eliot, son of Harvard president Charles William Eliot. Davis spent a few weeks with the Champlain Society, as the young men called themselves, and later reported on their geologic findings to the Boston Society of Natural History. Davis reported that glacial action was conspicuous over the whole island:

The mountain summits are all rounded, and when protected from weathering, sometimes show polishing or striation: boulders of foreign rocks are common even on the summits. Along the shore, the drift shows well scratched pebbles and boulders, and is therefore probably of original, unstratified, subglacial origin, somewhat modified in surface form by the sea during its former higher level . . . During a time of colder climate, there was an invasion of the region from the north by a sheet of ice, such as that which still maintains possession of Greenland.

Davis also described "beds of stratified clay bearing marine fossils" at various points on the lowland of the island and the mainland, up to about two hundred feet above the present sea level.

Geologists who visited later, including George Stone (1899), Florence Bascom (1919), and Edward Raisz (1929), noted the presence of this "cove clay" at the south end of Jordan Pond, along Hunter's Brook and other stream valleys, and beneath many wetlands. They found fossils of arctic marine fauna buried in the mud, suggesting an ocean of a cooler climate.

These marine features became stranded when the ice finally receded from interior Maine and the land rebounded, causing sea levels to drop dramatically. This "lowstand" was brief, geologically speaking, only about five hundred years or so. The land relaxed, and the sea, swollen with meltwater, began to rise again, quickly at first, then more slowly. The tidal marshes at Northeast Creek and Bass Harbor Marsh developed. In the cove between Great Head and Otter Point, fragments of shells began to accumulate, broken pieces of marine creatures that died thousands of years ago, now the tan sands of Sand Beach.

The continued, gradual rise of global sea level brought the ocean close to its present position about three thousand years ago. It has been rising ever since.

Florence Bascom at the height of her career, early twentieth century. *THE STONE LADY* BY I. F. SMITH

Acadia's geology was a foundational element in creation and promotion of the park. Bar Harbor resident and park founder George Dorr noted, "The character of this coast and its extraordinary fitness to great recreational needs are due to glacial action." In 2010 the author of a park inventory of geological resources wrote, "Acadia National Park preserves one of the premier places in the world to observe evidence of such dramatic crustal rebound and sea level changes."

To observe Acadia's rock formations is to witness fire and ice, rain and wind. The forces of time continue to work against the foundations of Acadia. Sea level continues to rise, and the Atlantic surf continues to crash against the granite shoreline, gradually eroding softer rock. Two miles east of Day Mountain, at Monument Cove, the ocean tumbles boulders into smooth spheres at the foot of blocky reddish cliffs. A piece of the cliff has become separated, a towering stack at the ocean's edge. Storm waves push boulders onto the roads, and perhaps into new caves forming at Ironbound Island and the Schoodic Peninsula. The soft gray marine clay, what's left of the ancient DeGeer Sea, slumps and washes away.

Shifts continue below the earth's surface, too. In 2006 a series of earthquakes rocked Acadia. The strongest, a magnitude 4.2, sent "megablocks" of Cadillac Mountain granite sliding down the side of Dorr and Champlain Mountains and opening new fractures in the bedrock. The tremors revealed the presence of a fault beneath Frenchman Bay off Bar Harbor. More than that, they were a reminder that Acadia continues to be shaped and reworked. Even the bedrock is temporary.

Like ruins in the jungle, old caves and sea cliffs became obscured by trees and the forest floor, their consistent occurrence at 220 to 230 feet above sea level a clue to their dramatic past. The sea stack on Day Mountain was well known to nineteenth-century ramblers in Acadia, who knew it as Pulpit, Tilting, or Chimney Rock. The triangular block of granite on the top is loose, and today is in a different position than Nathaniel Shaler showed in his illustrations.

In 1922 vandals toppled the uppermost stone, and the Seal Harbor Path Committee (likely helped by John D. Rockefeller Jr.) brought in a crane along the trail (now abandoned) to reset the stone. Why was it so

The sea-worn beach and cliff at Monument Cove. C. SCHMITT

important that the formation be restored? The name *pulpit* conjures a raised platform where a priest or minister stands when leading a worship service: What lesson might be preached from a granite column in the forest sublime?

Haunted by histories of flood and ice, people come to Acadia for a thousand different reasons; their experiences are as varied as the landscape. But most seem to be looking for something that can be found where rocks meet the sea.

Scenery

The Evolution and Allure of Acadia's Diverse Flora

It is obvious that we live in the midst of a unique and precious landscape with horticultural treasures that require vigilant protection and support.

—Judith Goldstein, *Majestic Mount Desert II*

In the hollow between Penobscot and Sargent Mountains, a forest of gray-green weathered spruce surrounds a small pond. Slow-growing, exposed to harsh winds, fog, and snow, some of the trees are hundreds of years old, somehow surviving in the thin layer of soil accumulated atop the granite. The pond and the woods feel ancient, but this is a young landscape, having emerged only since the last ice sheet melted away.

Like the rocks that reveal the island's molten, shattered, frozen, and flooded past, the land cover also tells something of the island's history. Upon the blank template left by the glaciers came lake and stream, tundra and forest, meadow and marsh, in a sequence that reveals how the climate of Acadia changed over the last fifteen thousand years, creating a unique and diverse assembly of ecosystems.

In just a few miles of terrain, where elevation ranges from sea level to more than one thousand feet, beaches, salt marshes, and tidal pools lie at the foot of subalpine summits. Ponds formed in granite bowls. The layer of ocean mud deposited during postglacial times created areas of poor drainage, leading to the formation of wetlands. Bogs thick with several meters of peat occur next to rocky coastal cliffs.

Acadia's coastal location means that the waters of the Gulf of Maine temper summer and winter temperatures, creating cool, wet conditions with frequent rain and summer fog, although Acadia receives more precipitation in winter than in summer. The ocean keeps Isle au Haut a bit warmer, with less snow and fog, than the larger Mount Desert Island and the mainland.

Acadia lies in the center of Maine's coastal climate zone; in just three degrees of latitude, the state contains the same climate gradient as twenty degrees of latitude in Europe, a distance approximately twice the length of California. The result is a much greater range in environments, and greater plant diversity, than is the case in most similarly sized regions of the world. At less than a hundred square miles, Acadia National Park encompasses less than 1 percent of the state's total land area, but hosts more than half of the different ecosystems found in Maine and more than one thousand plant species.

Sargent Mountain Pond illustrates this evolution of the landscape. At 1,050 feet, it is the second-highest summit in the Mount Desert range. Given its elevation and location relative to the receding ice sheet, Sargent Mountain Pond is believed to be Maine's "first" lake.

How did rock, scraped bare by glaciers, become a pond?

Sixteen thousand years ago, Sargent Mountain was a nunatak, an island of rock surrounded by ice (and then seawater, as the ocean chased the glaciers northward). Between two bare peaks, a depression filled with meltwater and occasional rain. Silty particles washed in from the surrounding granite. This rock "flour" contained minerals, including phosphorus, a nutrient required by plants. Diatoms, single-celled algae encased in microscopic shells of glass-like silica, were the first arrivals, blown in on the wind or carried by birds and insects.

As the ice disappeared from lower elevations, over thousands of years, tundra vegetation spread north: sedges, willows, grasses, alders and dwarf birches, and ferns. Lots of ferns.

Trees—poplar, spruce, paper birch, and white and jack pine—arrived through lowland corridors, reaching the exposed summits of Mount Desert as the ancestors of today's Wabanaki peoples entered the region, hunting caribou, musk ox, and mammoth across the ferny tundra. By

Sargent Mountain Pond. C. SCHMITT

the time southern New England and the Maine coast, including Acadia, were ice-free, shrubby willows, birches, sedges, and other plants had taken root on the mountain slopes.

The period from fifteen thousand to ten thousand years ago was one of great and lasting change. This period included the dramatic drop in sea level due to rebound of the land surface, and a brief return to glacial conditions when temperatures cooled as abruptly as they had warmed (the Younger Dryas event), plunging Acadia back to glacial conditions. The Younger Dryas cold lasted for a thousand years.

Rapid warming 11,600 years ago ended the Younger Dryas. Acadia was four degrees warmer than today, with less rain and snow. Lake levels dropped. Shrub fens and spruce-scattered tundra dried out into mixed forests of hemlock, white pine, birch, maple, and beech. Fire became more frequent, fueling the growth of jack pine and white pine higher up the hillsides. The expanding forests restricted caribou habitat.

At the same time, sea levels rose, and the Gulf of Maine basin formed. Twice-daily tides mixed the warm surface layers with cold layers below, lowering surface water temperatures and causing fog to form. Increased moisture favored spruce and fir over pine and hemlock—but only along a narrow band near the shore that included Acadia's coastal islands and peninsulas.

While in the rest of Maine, spruce and fir have dominated the forest for only the last five hundred years, at Acadia spruce persisted for some five thousand years. This dominant "maritime spruce-fir" community is on display at Sargent Mountain Pond. But so many other ecosystems are here, too. Acadia's geographic and geologic histories placed it within a broad transition zone between temperate ecosystems to the south and boreal ecosystems to the north.

Within a few hours' walk from Sargent Mountain Pond are the red pine forests of Norumbega and Eliot Mountains and white cedar woodlands growing in the shadows of Pemetic and the Bubbles. In one part, the cedars are dry and acidic, with heathlike shrubs; in another, cedar and ash tilt this way and that over thin, wet soils. These cedar groves grow nowhere else in Maine.

Across the Jordan Valley, jack pines cling to the summit of Cadillac Mountain. The most northern American pine, jack pine survived the ice age at low elevations in the Appalachian and Ozark Mountains of the Southeast. From these refugia, jack pine was able to reestablish across the northern tier of the United States, taking root in areas cleared by the glacier. Individual trees live briefly, only a hundred years or so, but they proliferate when young or when fire opens their seritonous cones. An older jack pine forest stands fast on the open, sunny crest of Schoodic Head Mountain.

Several other boreal species reach the southern extent of their ranges at Acadia, plants with magical names like beachhead iris, marsh felwort, blinks, baked-apple berry, roseroot stonecrop, leafybract aster, and dwarf Canadian primrose.

Meanwhile, sometimes on the very same hills, are species at the northern edge of their range: pitch pine, oak, butternut, mountain laurel, and dogwood. The large, fragrant, pink-purple flowers of thimbleberry bloom in Acadia, and one-sided rush sprouts from cracks in summit ledges. Swamp azalea and water-willow fringe the lakes.

Few species are everywhere; north and south mix and match, growing in hollows or isolated ledges.

Twenty percent of Acadia's plant species are considered officially rare, threatened, or endangered; six species are globally rare. Alpine or Appalachian fir clubmoss, smooth sandwort, boreal blueberry, and neglected reedgrass root in the shadows of pitch and jack pines on Cadillac Mountain. Other rare species are small, inconspicuous plants of peatlands and the edges of cold, clear lakes: screwstem, quillwort, Pickering's reedgrass. As a national park, Acadia affords the protection necessary for many of these species to persist.

Just as geologists came to study Acadia's exposed granite surfaces and rock formations, botanists and flower enthusiasts explored the diversity of flora.

One of the earliest botanists to visit Acadia was Louise Helen Coburn of Skowhegan, Maine, who was also a poet and historian. The second woman graduate of Colby College and a trained botanist, Coburn was editor of the *Maine Naturalist* and president of the Josselyn Botanical Society. She returned often to the island, locating, identifying, gathering, and pressing plants into specimens, which were later placed in herbarium collections, as was the practice of the day.

Botanical collecting made a major advance with the work of the Champlain Society, a group of Harvard students who began spending their summers camping on the island and conducting natural history surveys in the 1880s. Directed by Charles Eliot, son of Harvard president Charles W. Eliot, Champlain Society members focused on finding new species as they compiled a list of the island's vegetation. They made repeated excursions to Mount Desert's summits, including Sargent Mountain, which was usually an all-day trip via the gorge or Hadlock Ponds.

While membership in the club—and scientific commitment— varied over the years, the Botanical Department, under the leadership of Edward Lothrup Rand, remained the most robust. By 1885 it was left to Rand and Charles Eliot to carry on the serious work of the Champlain

Society, including (as they wrote in their logbooks) "the exploration of Harbor Brook Valley and the Amphitheatre as well as that part of Sargent Mountain around the Lake of the Clouds."

After graduation, Rand continued to work on his vegetation lists, engaging volunteers from across Mount Desert Island to help compile a complete plant inventory, published in 1894 as *Flora of Mount Desert Island, Maine.*

Champlain Society "captain" Charles Eliot developed a different relationship with plants: He apprenticed with pioneering landscape architect Frederick Law Olmsted and became a designer of gardens and parks across the United States. Around the same time, landscape architect Ernest Bowditch was founding his Point Lookout Club on Isle au Haut. They are among several connections between gardens, landscape design, and Acadia.

❦

The trail south from Sargent Mountain Pond descends to Birch Spring, rambles over the south ridge of Cedar Swamp Mountain, and then flattens out and widens. Salt air drifts through the forest. Suddenly, a tall gate appears, images of mythical plants and animals carved into the thick, polished cedar. The gate leads into a garden next to Thuya Lodge, the historic home of landscape gardener and engineer Joseph Henry Curtis.

Curtis had deep-set eyes; in later years he added a beard to his graying mustache. He loved three things above all: hard cider, tobacco, and the wild beauty of Mount Desert Island. A Civil War veteran, Curtis worked with Olmsted in 1872 but was largely self-taught. In 1880 he bought twenty acres from the Savage family and built the first of several homes, thus becoming one of the first summer residents of Northeast Harbor. Though based in Boston, he designed many properties in Maine, including a summer colony on Hancock Point, Spruce Point Road in Boothbay, Kebo Racetrack, High Head, and the Joseph Bowen garden at Hulls Cove in Mount Desert.

After the death of his wife in 1913, he put more energy into path-making and completed a final house at the top of the hill in 1916, inspired by the cabin architecture of Augustus Savage along the trail to

Jordan Pond. He planted an apple orchard (to support the cider habit) and a garden with bee balm and Scotch roses. He built a studio where his son Henry could practice piano (Henry died in 1918). For a time an elderly couple lived in a downstairs back room and served as housekeepers. Alone, Curtis encouraged his visitors to arrive via the path and join him in a smoke or a drink; he made fun of "grim puritans."

Curtis ate his lunch outside along the terraces and usually had dinner at the Asticou Inn, where proprietor Charles Savage had become a good friend. After a night of food, drink, and talk, Curtis would light his pipe and walk home, lantern in hand, its single candle flickering up the dark terraces.

He valued privacy and quiet, yet welcomed others to the terraces, as long as they shared his respect for the environment. If anyone disturbed the peace or trampled plants, Curtis could react quite violently, posting accusatory notes such as: "Especial care must be taken not to break down the blackberry bushes. I have promised them protection, and if necessary shall exclude all Northeast Harbor rather than break my word and forfeit the respect of a single bush."

Curtis left Asticou Terraces, intended as a "botanical-scenic trust to be of enduring interest and benefit for the public," to the Town of Mount Desert when he died in 1928. Charles K. Savage took over as trustee, a position he would hold for thirty-seven years.

On the other side of the island lived Beatrix Farrand. Self-taught, a charter fellow of the American Society of Landscape Architects, Farrand informally apprenticed with Arnold Arboretum's Charles Sprague Sargent. She toured the gardens of Europe, started her own business, and designed hundreds of gardens, including the East Garden at the White House. An established landscape gardener by the time she inherited her family's Bar Harbor estate in 1917 at the age of forty-five, she converted Reef Point into a botanical garden, library, and horticultural experiment station. After years of trial and error, she finally began to view Acadia's acidic soil as an asset, a place where rhododendrons and azaleas would flourish. She was critical of lawns and exotic plants, and heeded Sargent's advice to "to make the plan fit the ground and not twist the ground to fit a plan."

Joseph Henry Curtis. ASTICOU TERRACES TRUSTEES REPORT,
NORTHEAST HARBOR LIBRARY

In the early 1920s Farrand worked with John D. Rockefeller Jr. to design his Seal Harbor estate garden; later in the decade she worked on carriage road edges using native plants, taking her cues from the surrounding natural areas. Farrand and her husband opened their home, library, and gardens to the public in August 1939 as a philanthropic and educational institution.

Others who collected plants at Acadia expressed their pleasure through botanical illustration. Charles Faxon drew for Charles Sprague Sargent's *Silva of North America*, Elsie L. Shaw for *How to Know the Wild*

Flowers, Kate Furbish for *The Flora of Maine*. Margaret Stupka, wife of Acadia's first naturalist, Arthur Stupka, detailed flowering plants and trees in the park's monthly newsletter, *Nature Notes*.

George Dorr, cofounder and first superintendent of Acadia National Park, had always viewed Acadia as a plant sanctuary, a scaled-up version of the gardens he created with his mother at their Bar Harbor home, Old Farm. Preserving the diversity of Acadia's flora and fauna was a key factor in its preservation as a park. "The area includes much forestland, with deep valleys which offer admirable shelter for wild life," Dorr wrote in *National Geographic*. It was "the best opportunity along the whole Maine coast for preserving and exhibiting in a single tract its native flora."

He found everything he needed to fulfill his vision in the few acres near the spring between Newport (Champlain) and Dry (Dorr) Mountains. He developed three "hardy garden walks" to the area from Bar Harbor. Dorr purchased the area in 1909 and made it the headquarters for the Wild Gardens of Acadia in December 1916. He wanted to work with the park to not only conserve Acadian flora and fauna, but also provide students, architects, and gardeners an opportunity to observe native plants growing under natural conditions. Dorr encouraged others to plant gardens and established the Mount Desert Nurseries, a commercial outlet that supplied residents with their gardening and landscaping needs.

———

The people who felt an urge to wall off, preserve, and protect Acadia's flora were reacting to changes in their surroundings. By the time Rand, Dorr, Farrand, Curtis, and the rest came to Mount Desert, Acadia's forests had already been altered by two centuries of manipulation, especially logging. European settlers first cut down the large white pines, which were in high demand for shipbuilding, and then the larger spruce trees. Smaller trees were milled into various wooden parts and pieces. Forest cover reached a low point between 1850 and 1875, but logging continued into the early 1900s.

Logging contributed to fires accidentally, when sparks from cigarettes or machinery ignited slash piles, and purposely when fires were set to clear land. While the Native people set fires, perhaps to increase the numbers of paper birch trees, which they valued highly, burning was not used as extensively in the Acadia region as it was by tribes to the south and west. Studies of charcoal and pollen layers in the Bowl, a small pond near the Beehive, suggest that European settlers increased the frequency of fires above the natural, 100- to 150-year fire cycle.

Visitors, too, created fires: Residents of Isle au Haut attributed a large, two-month fire in the 1870s to blueberry pickers camping out on the island.

In the early 1900s logging on Mount Desert shifted, targeting smaller spruce and fir suitable for making pulp and paper. Fires were less common, in part because Bar Harbor enacted "slash laws," and the establishment of the national park resulted in improved fire patrol procedures. But the island's vegetation had been affected.

Fire at a lumber camp on the south shore of Jordan Pond burned the mature trees and the soil on the south slopes of Pemetic and Penobscot Mountains. Fire had destroyed the hotel atop Green (Cadillac) Mountain; vegetation quickly reclaimed the carriage road and cog railway.

Widespread cutting and burning created greater patchiness and stands of even-aged trees, a change noted by ecologists Barrington Moore and Norman Taylor in their paper, *Vegetation of Mount Desert Island, Maine, and its Environment*. They attributed the abundance of pitch pine on Mount Desert Island to fire:

Pitch pine, a picturesque tree, but of no value here since it seldom reaches sufficient size to be worth sawing into even low grade lumber, has most probably increased in areas since the arrival of the white man. This is because the barren rocky places on which it will grow, but where other trees are unable to survive, have been considerably increased by human interference, chiefly by fires."

Moore had earlier described the distinctiveness of Acadia's scenery:

The island is what is known to scientists as a tension point or meeting point between different plant and animal habitats. Such places have a

*peculiar fascination for the scientist in that they afford unusual oppor-
tunities for studying, among other things, the relation of plants and
animals to their environment, matters of much practical importance
in farming, in forestry, in horticulture and many other pursuits. Here
it is primarily a meeting of north and south, in which the north seems
to be the present master, but the south strongly represented. From the
forestry point of view I can state that on no area of size have I seen
growing together forests representing such different conditions and
consequently with such different requirements . . . The forests of Mt.
Desert Island represent a stretch of country extending from Labrador
to southern New Jersey.*

He also agreed with George Dorr that conserving the scenery was
important for advancing knowledge of the world:

*Scientists all over America are urging the preservation of natural
areas for scientific study. In research on distribution, on the influence
of environment upon plants and animals, and on adaptation, it is
essential to have areas on which the flora and fauna can be found
undisturbed by outside agencies. The creation of the Lafayette [Acadia]
National Park on an island of such great interest as Mount Desert
Island is, therefore, of the utmost importance to science.*

Dorr couldn't get the funds to fully develop the Wild Gardens, but
he used the organization to develop communities of gardeners, educate
the public about Acadia's natural landscape, and preserve the island scenery. Citing Sargent's *Silva* often, Dorr wrote in *The Acadian Forest*, "As
a botanical area Mount Desert Island is singularly rich . . . The natural
growth will henceforth be protected and cared for within the national
park bounds and restored where needful till it shall represent completely,
as in a wild botanic garden, the whole Acadian region."

Dorr envisioned the park, then, not just as a place to protect and
study plants, but also as a place to restore scenery. In the 1920s he provided funds for Philadelphia geologist-chemist-botanist Edgar Wherry
to come to Acadia to survey and photograph the park's plants. Wherry

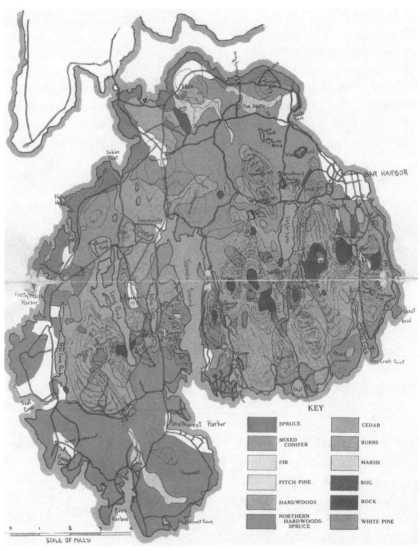

KEY

	SPRUCE		CEDAR
	MIXED CONIFER		BURNS
	FIR		MARSH
	PITCH PINE		BOG
	HARDWOODS		ROCK
	NORTHERN HARDWOODS-SPRUCE		WHITE PINE

SCALE OF MILES

Vegetation map of Mount Desert Island, showing forest types as mapped by Barrington Moore and Norman Taylor, 1927. *VEGETATION OF MOUNT DESERT ISLAND, MAINE AND ITS ENVIRONMENT*, BROOKLYN BOTANIC GARDEN MEMOIRS, VOL. III, COURTESY BROOKLYN BOTANIC GARDEN

was on leave from the US Department of Agriculture's Bureau of Chemistry, and his work focused on the distribution and cultivation of native plants. He worked with Barrington Moore to study the influence of soils on plant distribution and published an article dedicated to the wood ferns of Mount Desert Island. In 1928 the Garden Club of Mount Desert published one thousand copies of Wherry's resulting book, *Wild Flowers of Mount Desert Island, Maine*, which quickly sold out.

The national conservation movement that had expanded during Teddy Roosevelt's presidency continued to have influence. Citizens joined the effort to protect and restore Acadia's native plants. During the Depression, Civilian Conservation Corps (CCC) crews, assisted by Acadia National Park's resident landscape architect, Benjamin Breeze, established seedling nurseries to grow native plants for revegetating areas after trail construction, using transplanted oak, spruce, and pine from John D. Rockefeller Jr.'s property. Members of the Bar Harbor Garden Club sponsored a campaign for the protection of wildflowers and shrubs on Mount Desert Island, and plans were made to save some of the rare and endangered flower species.

On October 21, 1947, a forest fire began on the northeastern side of Mount Desert, and over the next four weeks, it swept across the eastern half of the island, burning more than one quarter of the island, including much of Bar Harbor. More than two hundred year-round and summer families lost their homes. It was the most extensive fire in recent memory, and had a lasting impact on Bar Harbor and the island's vegetation. The eastern side of Isle au Haut burned at the same time, one of many fires across the state during the "Year Maine Burned."

Sargent Mountain did not burn, and the forest surrounding Sargent Mountain Pond reflects the underlying soil, built up over centuries. The same is true on the western side of Mount Desert, on Western and Bernard Mountains, where old-growth spruce-fir forests are draped with aged broom moss. On the most exposed summits, wind pruned mature spruce and fir into krummholz: twisted, wizened, stout forms. Pockets of uncut forest persist on Isle au Haut and Schoodic.

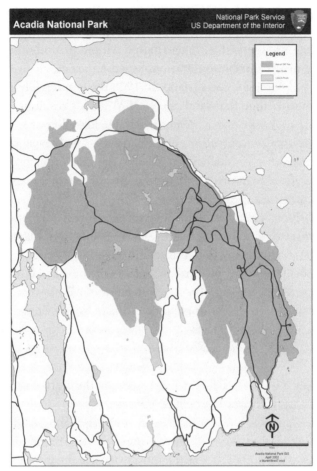

Area of Mount Desert Island burned by 1947 fire.
ACADIA NATIONAL PARK

In the burned areas, stands of white birch, aspen, oak, and red maple flourished where conifers had grown before. The profound transformation of the scenery prompted people to make changes, too.

Acadia landscape gardener Beatrix Farrand believed that "surroundings deserve to be the solace of the poor more than the playground of the rich." Though she designed private gardens, her goal was always to make plants and garden design accessible. But Bar Harbor was a different place after "The Fire." Farrand, who also was struggling with the mounting costs of the Reef Point property, decided to abandon her home in 1955. She gave the library to the University of California at Berkeley, demolished her family's cottage, and dismantled the gardens.

Some of the plants were salvaged by Charles Savage, whose grandfather Augustus founded the Asticou Inn in 1883. Savage was not a professional landscape architect, but like other members of his family, he was well educated and interested in a range of intellectual pursuits. At the time Farrand was dissolving Reef Point, Savage managed the Asticou Inn and Jordan Pond House. A lover of native plants and a student of Japanese garden design, he decided to preserve the plant collection of Beatrix Farrand. With financial support from John D. Rockefeller Jr., Savage purchased the trees and shrubs for five thousand dollars and built the Asticou Azalea Garden and the Thuya Garden in Northeast Harbor in the mid-1950s.

He built the Azalea Garden across from the Asticou Inn, on the site of a swamp described as "dormant" and "unsightly," an "eyesore." Out of this "unappetizing setting" Savage distilled the woods and craggy mountaintops of Acadia into a water garden inspired by the Katsura Imperial Villa in Kyoto. Farrand's prize azaleas and rhododendrons, the largest collection in the United States, were replanted along the newly sculpted paths and glades.

At Thuya, which Joseph Curtis had left under Savage's care, Rockefeller gave 110 acres to enlarge the preserve (from the original 20 acres) and funds for Savage to develop it. Savage designed gardens that would complement a public botanical library created in the Lodge. He planted perennial flower beds in the old apple orchard, with more of Farrand's azaleas and spruces along the woodsy edges.

Savage worked hard to interpret and fulfill Curtis's vision, writing in an unpublished report on the Asticou Terraces, "In this extremely complex, harassing mode of present day high-pressure existence there can never be enough opportunities for quiet recreation—a situation which Curtis seemed to foresee."

Savage recognized the parallels between Maine and Japanese landscapes: bold ledges, rocks, and pines. Acadia's woods, mountains, and

Charles Savage.
NORTHEAST HARBOR LIBRARY

shorelines evoke east Asia: strewn boulders, blankets of moss, brilliant autumnal color, a patina of past seasons and eons. A spiritual energy surrounds the omnipresent rock. At both Asticou and Thuya, it can be hard to tell where the garden ends and wild nature begins. Wooden gates, mowed paths, raked sand, and pristine moss carpets—what Savage would call "harmonious embellishments"—are clues that one has strayed into a designed and carefully maintained scene.

And yet, just beyond the gate, the woods grow as they will.

Gardening is a dialogue with the landscape—a way to engage with it more deeply. Instead of searching for, identifying, and collecting plants like a botanist, the gardener moves plants, rearranging them to his or her own design, yet compelled all the while by nature. Gardeners attempted to re-create the essence and structure of Acadia's real landscape.

As a Japanese gardening manual famously put it, gardeners should "heed the request of the stone" when arranging rocks. How and where a stone is placed is a response to the gardener's experience of natural objects and places—beaches on which stones are found, mountains from which they have tumbled. The placing of the stone affects further experience of the natural environment—by, for example, echoing a distant, previously inconspicuous hill. The meaning of this subtle but detectable balance between the natural and the contrived was elusive, yet irresistible to the gardeners of Acadia.

Acadia's setting and natural beauty gave strength and value to the work of landscape professionals like Curtis, Farrand, and Savage, while allowing nonexperts the chance to experience and contemplate such beauty. Farrand, for example, described in her *Reef Point Gardens Bulletin* how she wanted to show "what outdoor beauty can contribute to those who have the interest and perception that can be influenced by trees and flowers and open air composition."

Acadia's scenery is not that far from the human concept of a "garden." A formal garden looks out of place in a landscape already considered Eden by many. Yet settlers derived the term "Eden," the original name for Bar Harbor, not from the biblical paradise but a sixteenth-century English statesman and alchemist named Richard Eden. The son of a cloth merchant, Eden translated Spanish accounts of the New World into English, encouraging colonialism.

It is easy, though, to favor the other Eden. Throughout recorded history, visitors, summer residents, and year-round inhabitants all praised Acadia's Edenic qualities. Borns and Maasch cite physician-geologist John DeLaski who wrote, "I cannot conceive of any earthly scenery so well adapted to suggest and develop the nobler aspirations of the soul, as a landscape where the mountains and the sea are thus blended into intimate friendship."

Many had a utopian view of Acadia, a universe unto itself, an island paradise remote in place and time, "beyond the destructive grasp

Asticou Azalea Garden. C. SCHMITT

of mankind," as John Gillis wrote in *Islands of the Mind.* If elsewhere Earth's finer qualities had been lost, perhaps at Acadia they could at least be preserved and replicated. Utopians have a tendency to repair what has been broken, to replace what is lost. And so, after the devastation of the fire of 1947, the people got to work.

Savage built his gardens. Betty Thorndike and Janet TenBroeck, members of the Bar Harbor Garden Club, began making George Dorr's wild garden dream a reality. Acadia's superintendent, Harold Hubler, offered them a three-quarter-acre plot at Sieur de Monts to grow and display wildflowers, which would be looked after by club members. Although the plot was covered with blackberry bushes and fire-damaged maples, there were plenty of large ferns and a winding brook fed by the spring. The Wild Gardens of Acadia committee, composed of members of area garden clubs and other interested gardeners, began laying out walkways and divided the gardens into areas simulating natural plant communities. The National Park Service helped with paths, labels, and hauling rock so the mountain habitat might be more authentic in an otherwise rock-less site.

The gardeners decided to include only those species indigenous to Acadia. Guided by Wherry's *Wild Flowers*, volunteers established more than four hundred native plants. How would they feel to learn that since their efforts, 241 plant species have disappeared from Acadia and nearly a third of the park's flora consists of nonnative, sometimes invasive species like lupine, rugosa rose, and purple loosestrife? Or that development for new homes has continued to gnaw away at the forest, and trampling and unofficial trails have damaged alpine vegetation?

The flora of Acadia may have changed, but its character has not. One can still experience blooming tidal pools and shimmering salt marsh grasses, lush meadows and towering forests, alpine scrub and mountain pond lilies, all in a single day. It can be overwhelming, so beautiful it hurts. Perhaps that is why so many have searched for specific plants to identify and collect, or dug their hands into the soil to cultivate and arrange the vegetation, capturing to keep from being crushed by the beauty of their surroundings.

Gathering

The First People of Acadia

We succeeded. We are still here. Our culture and languages are alive and well.

—GEORGE NEPTUNE, PASSAMAQUODDY AND
ABBE MUSEUM EDUCATOR

AT THE EDGE OF DOWNTOWN BAR HARBOR, TWICE EACH DAY, THE TIDE drops low enough to expose beaches, mudflats, and a bar of sand that leads out across the harbor to Bar Island. On a Saturday in July, drumbeats echo across the mudflats. *Thump. Thump. Thump.* Men's voices chant with the rhythm beat by many hands. *Thump. Thump. Thump.* The Burnurwurbskek Singers, members of the Penobscot Indian Nation, send their songs into the crowd assembled for the annual Native American Festival and Basketmakers Market on the campus of College of the Atlantic in Bar Harbor.

The basketmakers sit behind rows of tables, working on their craft. They weave splints of brown ash, a tree that grows along streams and floodplains. Some dye the white-blonde wood different colors; others give each strip a twist during the weave, creating a fancy "porcupine" basket; still others incorporate braids of fragrant sweetgrass or other fibers. Potential customers, the interested, and the curious peruse the art on display. To some, the baskets may appear to be just a high-quality craft, a pretty container, an investment. But each ash tree cut, felled, stripped, pounded, split, bent, and woven into form continues a deep connection with Acadia held by members of the Native American tribes in Maine— Micmac, Maliseet, Penobscot, and Passamaquoddy.

Low tide reveals the bar to Bar Island, or "clam gathering place." C. SCHMITT

The word *Wabanaki* (or *Waponahki*) derives from the Algonquian words *waban* ("light" or "white," referring to the dawn in the east) and *aki* ("land") and means People of the Dawn, for Acadia is the region where the first light of day touches the continent; for part of the year, the first light falls upon Cadillac Mountain.

The summer gathering is something the Wabanaki have been doing forever, drawn by Acadia's diverse resources, pleasant climate, and beauty. The current event, held annually since 1989, is jointly sponsored by the Maine Indian Basketmakers Alliance and the Abbe Museum, an independent, nonprofit organization and the first Smithsonian Affiliate in the state of Maine. The Abbe represents the continuum of ancient to modern Wabanaki presence in Acadia, the result of Native American activism and involvement that led to changes in how museums care for their collections and present them to the public.

In the early 2000s the museum renovated a former YMCA building in downtown Bar Harbor to create seventeen thousand square feet of

Molly Neptune Parker, Passamaquoddy, selling her baskets at the 2013 Native American Festival. FROM THE COLLECTION OF THE ABBE MUSEUM, BAR HARBOR, MAINE

exhibition galleries, indoor and outdoor program spaces, a research lab, and state-of-the-art storage for the largest and best-documented collection of Maine Indian basketry. A Native Advisory Council, appointed by tribal leaders, provides insight and ideas regarding the museum's strategic direction and operations.

Yet this inclusion and collaboration with the Wabanaki began only recently, in the 1980s.

The baskets tell the history of the tribes and their efforts to maintain their culture and sovereignty, efforts which have been consistent throughout time but intensified in the 1970s, when the Wabanaki began to pursue historic treaty rights through a series of unprecedented legal actions and joined the momentum of the national Indian rights movement. Foreshadowing today's basketmakers' market, in 1979 they participated in the Pride of Maine Fair held at the College of the Atlantic: dancing, playing music, making baskets, and demonstrating traditional cooking and medicinal practices. Participating tribal members found that baskets turned ash into a vessel to keep their stories, and basket sales became a portal into conversations about political struggles and injustices.

The basketmakers also contributed to the tradition of creating "collectors items," many of which ended up at museums, including the Abbe, where museum curators started working with local Natives in the middle of the twentieth century to document their collections of Wabanaki works, artifacts, and stories and expand the museum's scope to include ethnographic materials.

But the museum focused exclusively on the past. Historians and anthropologists assumed that "traditional" Native American cultures were vanishing, and they felt a duty to preserve, through collecting, what they believed would soon be lost.

Many of the objects in the collections were donated in the period during and after the Great Depression, when the market for baskets shrank. In 1931 Mary Cabot Wheelwright, founder of the Wheelwright Museum of the American Indian in Santa Fe, New Mexico, donated an important collection of Native American baskets and other objects. This was a significant addition to the original collection of precontact tools that New York physician Robert Abbe purchased from a Bar Harbor shop in 1926.

Many artifacts were dug out of the great piles of discarded shells, or middens, left by Wabanaki over the millennia. Archaeologists mapped nearly a hundred shell middens in Maine in the late nineteenth and early twentieth centuries and excavated only a small percentage. More than 625 sites would eventually be mapped along the coast from Little Deer Isle to Gouldsboro Bay, a visual reminder of the extent and intensity of human presence at Acadia. Thousands of fish bones, shells, sea mammal remains, swordfish points, hooks, beads, flutes, combs, and stone tools are more tangible reminders.

To house and display the tools, Abbe constructed a small building near Sieur de Monts Spring, within the national park but privately operated. It was the first institution in Maine to support archaeological research, although at the time the field was still young and undisciplined, with little regard for the destruction of places that might have been important to living Wabanaki. The purpose of the Lafayette National Park Museum of Stone Age Antiquities, Abbe wrote, was to collect and preserve local material found on and about Mount Desert Island, the "indestructible evidence of a vanished race." The museum accepted other collections of artifacts and sponsored excavations of Frenchman Bay shell middens.

"Introducing the collection of Stone Age Implements will stand for the epitome of the beauty and wonder of nature on the Eastern Continental coast," Abbe wrote. His small collection was "a brief but perfect incident in the path of the maddening crowds." He felt that the appeal of the artifacts, their historical drama, required a degree of ignorance and mystery that would dissolve after too much study by archaeologists. Certainly, he saw no relation to the Wabanaki who shared his Acadia home.

It took some time for the Wabanaki to develop their tourist trade, and throughout the nineteenth and twentieth centuries they had to reaffirm their existence, as many people (from Maine and from away) assumed all the Indians had long ago disappeared.

Many Indians worked in local fish plants, lumber camps, or farms, but to Acadia's maddening crowds of tourists, they were gypsies and vagabonds, last vestiges of a disappearing culture. They were conspicuous, given their habit of establishing temporary villages in Acadia, called "encampments" by white people. Up until about 1920, many lived seasonally in an encampment, a cluster of tents and wooden shacks at the southern edge of Bar Harbor, near Cromwell Stream on the east side of Ledgelawn Avenue. The summer encampment was subjected to increasing regulation with each passing year and pushed back farther and farther. The camp was displaced from the foot of Bar, or Bridge, Street by wharves and hotels and the Village Improvement Association, and then banned completely from the Bar Harbor shoreline.

Most Indians supplemented their income by making and selling items such as brooms, barrel staves, moccasins, and utility baskets. As more tourists began coming to Acadia, the Wabanaki found an emerging market for "specialty" baskets of ash splints and sweetgrass, porcupine

Clara Neptune, Penobscot, with baskets, ca. 1920.
F.H. ECKSTORM/FOGLER LIBRARY

quillwork, birch bark toys, and other crafts. They also sold sealskins, seagull breasts, snowshoes, carved paddles, and, to the lucky few, full-size birch bark canoes. Just as Acadia was an escape for urbanites, it was a place the Wabanaki could go to escape the industrialization surrounding their reservation lands while still continuing their culture.

Wabanaki encampment, Bar Harbor, ca. 1887. MAINE HISTORIC PRESERVATION COMMISSION

For a mobile and adaptive people, traveling to sell baskets was preferable to staying at home and farming, which is what government officials tried to get them to do, or working in a regimented factory. They sold baskets door-to-door, at train stations and boat landings, and from their tents. They gave canoe rides and lessons, and guided hunting and fishing trips. Fear and distrust of Indians was common in the nineteenth century, yet according to Passamaquoddy artist and educator George Neptune, "Eden provided a unique opportunity: the chance to interact and learn from Indians in a safe and trusting environment." Newspaper reporters and guidebook authors noted their presence, at times with disdain, such as this anonymous writer for *Frank Leslie's Illustrated Newspaper*:

> *One of the peculiar sights at Bar Harbor, the Maine Summer resort, is the encampment of the Passamaquoddy Indians, a little way from the West End Hotel, down on the shore. In thirty board shanties and tents live as many families of these relics of a great nation now dwindled . . . Every Summer they come to Bar Harbor in numbers of about one hundred and fifty, and tempt dollars from the tourists by*

their display of wonderfully-made baskets, miniature canoes, and all sorts of things. . . .

And Moses Foster Sweetser, in *Summer Days Down East,*

Near the village is an encampment of Penobscot Indians, tall, good-natured, lazy fellows, with plenty of gaudily-dressed squaws and pappooses, who make great numbers of baskets, canoes, and other barbaric curiosities, which are eagerly bought up by the visitors. Some of these half-French and entirely-Romish aborigines are among the best boatmen at Bar Harbor, and carry their delighted white patrons far out on the breezy bay in their light birch canoes.

The summer occupation of Acadia was a long-standing practice among people who did not view the landscape as a thing to own, buy, sell, or fence. Tribal members left their reservations at Old Town and Pleasant Point in early spring or late summer and came to Acadia as they had always done, setting up camp in Somesville, Southwest Harbor, and Bar Harbor, and in Blue Hill, Swan's Island, Deer Isle, and Isle au Haut.

Early in the morning, or later in the evening, when the camp storefronts closed down, the Wabanaki might have had time to pursue their own traditions or gather raw materials. In the spring they dug clams from the shallow cove of Bar Harbor. They speared salmon, lobsters, eels, and other fish from their canoes. They set fish weirs near the sandbar. They also hunted porpoise from their canoes, harvesting the animals for their valuable oil. Typically, they sold their extra catch at the town market or ship wharves and used the cash to purchase flour, molasses, blankets, hardware, and other goods.

They paddled over to the marshes in the harbors and islands to collect sweetgrass for basketmaking. Some of the grass was braided and dried so it could be used in smudging ceremonies and prayer fires. One inventory lists over 125 plant species in Acadia National Park and adjacent areas that the Wabanaki have used for food, materials, or medicine.

White birch was another important plant, with hundreds of uses. Folded and sewn with spruce or cedar roots, decorated with red and black dyed porcupine quills, and etched with double-curve designs, birch bark

Fancy porcupine-weave basket by Molly Molasses, Penobscot, 1862. FROM THE COLLECTION OF THE ABBE MUSEUM, BAR HARBOR, MAINE

became dishes, buckets, and other containers. Symbols etched into birch bark became a system for remembering ideas, a kind of language. "What the birch bark meant to them can hardly be understood by us. It gave them their canoes, their wigwams, their utensils, their kindling wood, their wrappings, their waterproofing," wrote historian Fannie Hardy Eckstorm.

The Wabanaki wove rushes and fibers of the "line tree," or basswood, into baskets, bags, and mats. Plants provided dyes: for blue, indigo; for red and pink, Solomon's seal fruits ("eel berries"), bloodroot, or blueberries; for green, white cedar and elm bark; for yellow, goldthread; for brown, alder bark.

Ash trees, pounded into splints, became baskets. Marketing baskets helped to keep alive the knowledge of how to make baskets, cultural uses for baskets, and the meanings of baskets.

Wabanaki encampment, Bar Harbor, 1881. KILBURN BROTHERS /
FROM THE COLLECTION OF THE ABBE MUSEUM, BAR HARBOR, MAINE

In order to market their products, the Wabanaki sometimes adopted customs from other Native American cultures, such as Plains Indian headdresses. To outsiders, such altering of tradition may have seemed like the Wabanaki were surrendering their identity, but giving the public what it wanted in order to sell tickets or baskets or hunting guide services instead helped to reaffirm their presence and distinctiveness as a culture. The act of creation only heightens the meaning of the final product.

Returning to Acadia every year, or even living there year-round, allowed the Wabanaki to continue a way of life in their ancestral homeland, despite incredible instability in their landscape and territory.

Between 1675 and 1783 the Wabanaki fought seven wars, conflicts resulting from the French, English, and Dutch colonists competing for land, resources, and profit of the coastal region, where Acadia was a strategic location.

War caused suffering beyond wounds, death, and destruction. Wabanaki survivors fled their homes to seek refuge with allies and neighbors. War interrupted seasonal subsistence patterns, preventing the Wabanaki from going to favorite hunting, fishing, and gathering places, including Acadia.

Before the wars began, the Wabanaki had already been devastated by foreign diseases brought by Europeans. Smallpox, cholera, and influenza killed more than 75 percent of the Wabanaki in the span of a few years (1616–19), a tragedy known as the Great Dying.

Conflict began when an Englishman from Virginia destroyed the Jesuit mission post at the mouth of Somes Sound, founded in 1613 at the Wabanaki's invitation opposite their seasonal village.

Several hundred Wabanaki lived year-round on Mount Desert Island, under the domain of chief Asticou, whose family was the center of one of the most important Wabanaki alliances encountered by early European visitors. The Europeans called him by the location he represented, *Astuwiku*, which means "it comes or grows together," a meeting place. Chief Asticou's name evokes wisdom and magic: *Asticou* also means a bowl-shaped depression in stone that held spiritual power.

Asticou's family was part of a larger community extending from the Narraguagus to the Penobscot. This regional group, headed by grand chief Bashaba of the Penobscot, was one of numerous populations of Native Americans speaking related Algonquian languages and dialects whose homeland extends from Newfoundland to northeastern Massachusetts.

Clad in moose hides and beaver fur, they built canoes and went to sea for fish, mammals, and seabird eggs. They followed the rivers north into the woods for more fish and game, and traveled east to the Machias and west to the Penobscot on snowshoes and sleds. At the harbor on the western shore of Isle au Haut, they hunted sea ducks during the August molting season. After netting the birds, they ate them fresh, or they salted or smoked them for later.

At the clambake place near the sandbar, *Ah-bays'auk*, people cooked clams over a fire or dried them by sun or smoke and packed them in *mik-nur-queh*, a birch bark box, for winter. *Ar-nass-cum-nal*, acorns, were also gathered in their season and dried. In the wintertime, a family wishing to have a fashionable dinner cooked the dried clams in water seasoned with bear or seal oil; after the clams were well soaked and boiled, pounded acorns were added to give it good flavor. Oysters were cooked and served the same way.

They excavated the outcrops of fine-grained volcanic rock, chipping and flaking the stone into tools. Where and when they had access to the sea and its resources, they settled year-round, including the coast of Acadia.

The Wabanaki also traveled extensively to trade with other groups. Acadia was an important place where extended family members would meet, gathering for political discussions, annual social gathering, and celebration. They traded baskets and birch bark containers, filled with corn from central and southern Maine, dried fish and berries from eastern Maine.

They had gathered there since the beginning.

After the final sheet of ice melted, around thirteen thousand years ago, and tundra grew across the raw earth, after migratory caribou and mastodon came to graze and fish arrived to spawn in fresh gravel streams, people followed. Highly skilled makers of stone tools and distinct fluted spear points, they came from the south and from the west, by land and perhaps by water, too.

As they neared the coast, they could see in the distance rounded summits rising above the watery horizon of the young ocean. They named the place *Peskamkuk*, the place to gather, hunt deer, spear fish, and trade; the place with a range of mountains, *Pemetic*; the highest mountain, the white mountain of the first light, *Wapuwoc*; the clam-digging place near the sandbar, *Moneskatik* (or *Man-es-ayd'ik*); the point of land to the east, *Eskwodek*. There were other islands, many islands, but *Peskamkuk* was the largest and—with fish in the water, game in the woods, clams along the shore, and beauty, so much beauty—most favorite.

Unlike most of North America's Native tribes, the Wabanaki were not forced to move or displaced from their traditional territories; they have always lived here, ever since the Creator, Glooskap (*Koluskap*) made them from the ash, as described by Tomah Joseph:

> *Glooskap came first of all into this country, into Nova Scotia, Maine, Canada, into the land of the Wabanaki, next to sunrise. There were no Indians here then (only wild Indians very far to the west) . . . And in this way he made Man: He took his bow and arrows and shot at trees, the basket-trees, the Ash. Then Indians came out of the bark of the Ash-trees.*

Advertisement

How Visitors from Near and Far Learned About a Place Called Acadia

One of the geographical and geological anvils on which the visual culture of the nation was forged is Mount Desert Island on the Maine Coast.

—JOHN WILMERDING, *THE ARTIST'S MOUNT DESERT*

BEYOND THE EDGE OF MOUNT DESERT ISLAND, TWENTY-FIVE MILES out to sea, is the remotest lighthouse in Maine. Since 1830, a light tower has warned anxious sailors away from the treeless island of Mount Desert Rock. Gannets plunge into the waves; gray seals and harbor seals bob and swim in the surf. Half of the island is submerged at high tide; the entire island is swallowed by waves during storms and hurricanes. Whale bones and other jetsam mix with the ruins of human occupation on the rock, everything weathered gray and crusted with guano. On the northern horizon, Mount Desert Island casts its striking silhouette of mountain and valley.

Both a treacherous obstacle to early sailors and a hopeful sign that land was near, Mount Desert Rock's combination of danger and redemption made it a worthy subject for artist Thomas Doughty, who painted the island and surrounding waters in 1836. Other painters would follow, drawn, as the Wabanaki were, to Acadia's rock formations, the sea crashing against mountains, and the mature forests. These early visitors—artists, naturalists, writers—promoted Acadia to their respective audiences, most of whom lived in cities.

The artists came in search of dramatic coastal scenes, ships dwarfed by crashing waves, settlements tucked between hills. With their old favorite places like Nahant, the Catskills, Niagara, and the White Mountains already getting crowded, they came in search of New England's remaining wilderness, and they found it on the coast of Maine.

Thomas Doughty's *Desert Rock Lighthouse, Maine* was the first image to reach a wide audience when it was exhibited at the Boston Athenaeum. The image was made into an engraving, issued as part of a series by George Virtue of London; in 1840 the print was one of thirty-three bound into a book, *American Scenery; or, Land, Lake and River Illustrations of Transatlantic Nature*.

Text by Nathaniel Willis accompanied each picture. "There is beautiful scenery in Maine, however," Willis assured his reader, "and Mr. Doughty, from one of whose pictures the accompanying drawing was taken, made a tour in search of it."

The engraver, William Radclyffe, embellished Doughty's original image with ships and a crew of shipwrecked sailors hauling a mast from the waves. Wrecks *were* common in the area, and Doughty himself similarly remade the image in a later painting, as did Currier & Ives, perhaps because it made for a better story, which according to Willis was expected of scenic places. So he wrote about a shipwreck in a storm. By showing and describing the presence of a newly constructed lighthouse station, Doughty and Willis also showed that Mount Desert was already becoming more approachable, both safer and easier to reach.

By the 1840s the Acadia region was popular among art buyers, with sketches of island views selling fast.

When Thomas Cole came to Mount Desert, in 1844, he was at the peak of his career as leader of the Hudson River School of landscape painting. Cole reflected and helped define the new attitude toward wilderness, one of attraction instead of fear. What began in the sixteenth and seventeenth centuries with scientific discoveries of a vast and complex universe had led to new thinking about the relationship between nature and God. By the nineteenth century, dramatic cliffs, high mountain summits, bare rock, and crashing waves prompted awe and fear because they provided glimpses of God—the sublime. Asymmetrical landscapes with

Engraved version of Thomas Doughty's *Desert Rock Lighthouse* that appeared in *American Scenery*, 1840. W. RADCLYFFE

tangled vegetation and rough textures weren't evil; they were *picturesque*, and more exciting than any old farm or city block. People saw the art and sought the same in the outdoors.

"Perhaps the most impressive characteristic of American scenery is its wildness," Cole wrote in his well-known "Essay on American Scenery." In civilized Europe, in contrast, "the primitive features of scenery have long since been destroyed or modified." American scenery was a blank slate, an empty page, a white canvas—a place where the visitor could find both the present *and* the future. The past (and its people) did not exist.

If nature was the source of America's distinctiveness as a culture and a nation, then any good American would want to see and know the nature of the country. For Cole, Mount Desert had the perfect combination of rugged wilderness and emerging civilization. It was accessible but unique among other New England resorts.

Cole made numerous sketches but mostly painted the cliffs of the eastern half of the island. In *Frenchman's Bay, Mount Desert Island, Maine*

(1845), a foamy green sea sweeps up the sides of dark, overhanging cliffs, and clouds linger in the near sky. The view seems to be from a rock at the sea's edge below the cliffs. Atop the cliff a sole figure, arms extended, faces the ocean to experience the sublime power of the waves against the granite.

Cole paid attention to rocks, like the pile of granite boulders in *Monument Rock near Sand Beach, Mount Desert*. He noticed the steep mountains, the basaltic appearance of vast bare walls of rock rising from the sea, as he traveled along the eastern shore of the island. Cole was preoccupied with erratic boulders, U-shaped valleys, gravel bars, and other phenomena then associated with the biblical Great Flood (but later shown to be glacial in origin).

Cole and his followers gained their appreciation for rocks, and glaciers, through their mingling with geologists, for theirs was a time when science was not so isolated, and artists, too, could be experts on the processes and transformations of nature. The landscape painters applied the day's scientific understanding through their art, while scientists needed artists to communicate their findings.

Charles T. Jackson's first report on the geology of Maine came with an atlas of illustrations by Franz (Francis) Graeter, who accompanied the surveying party. Advances in printing technology, combined with the new taste for scenery and its scientific explanations, increased the number of images in circulation.

For the exclusive few who cultivated an appreciation for landscape, knowledge of fine art and science was useful in social situations. Just as people in Boston, Philadelphia, and New York should be able to maintain a conversation about the picturesque, they should also be able to discuss the components of the picture: the makeup of the rocks, the species of tree, the sinuous shape of a river oxbow. To be among the exclusive, urban residents devoured published travel stories, attended scientific lectures, and viewed art exhibits. When they finally visited Acadia themselves, they looked for the scenes that famous artists had selected and approved for them.

It wasn't all a superficial ad campaign, a "cult of scenery." The concept of the picturesque gave people a way to talk about their experience of the landscape. For the first time, Westerners could express the feelings inspired by natural surroundings in an acceptable, even popular way. They could venture outside the garden gate and share the story of their adventure with family and friends.

— ⁓ —

Cole's painting *View Across Frenchman's Bay from Mount Desert Island, After a Squall*, went on view in New York at the National Academy of Design in 1845. Taking note were not just the scenery-loving public, but also fellow artists. Any landscape artist who was anyone, or wanted to be someone, now had to travel to Acadia, including Thomas Cole's student, Frederic Edwin Church.

Traveling to Acadia in 1850 in pursuit of dramatic seascapes, Church explored much of the same area sketched by his teacher and stayed at the same boardinghouse, the Lynam farm at Schooner Head. Church had already been promoting Appalachian scenery; he would do the same for Acadia.

In *Newport Mountain, Mount Desert* (1851), a man pulls vessel wreckage from the waves, in an echo of Thomas Doughty's revised images of Mount Desert Rock. The afternoon sun illuminates the reddish rocks along the shore; three other sailing vessels are on the horizon. In the background are the forested slopes and summit of Champlain Mountain. Church was able to capture the immensity of the Mount Desert hills, which loom much larger in reality than they appear on maps. The figures in Church's paintings of Acadia are appropriately overwhelmed.

His paintings, exhibited (and sold) in Pennsylvania and New York, placed the viewer more squarely in the scenery. Humans stand at ground level, rather than looking from afar or above. Church also created new English names for many of the island's prominent features, including Eagle Lake, the Beehive, and Summit Lake (Sargent Mountain Pond); like shipwrecked sailors, these names contributed to the "story" of the landscape.

Church strived to portray the rocks accurately, to capture the fading light of sunset or ocean-spray-filtered light. His involvement in science was even greater than Cole's. The texture, grain, hardness, color—all had to be accurate. Maine helped Church reach a new level in his art. When he saw the sun set over a lake in Acadia, and later painted it from memory in *Twilight in the Wilderness* (1860), he created what has been called one of the greatest paintings in the history of American art.

In an article in the *Bulletin of the American Art-Union*, Church described his visit, his exceeding delight with the scenery "and with the people, too." Mentioning the "fierce, frolicsome march of waves" crashing at Schooner Head, the "admirably varied outline" of the mountains, the "charms of scenery," he hinted at the opportunity for building hotels and providing for other "creature comforts." He foresaw Acadia's potential as a tourist destination.

During his return visits over the next twelve years, Church brought new visitors to Acadia. In 1855 he accompanied a crew of twenty-seven family and friends, including railroad lawyer Charles Tracy. In his now-legendary diary of the vacation, Tracy used the language of someone familiar with landscape painting and its geologic influence:

> *Mount Desert island appears at a great distance; at first, a pale line above the horizon, but gradually growing into a chain of hills, the most wild and picturesque, and as we drew in front of its south coast, the hills seemed to be divided and riven apart by deep cuts, going down to their foundations. Some were green with forests, & some were bald rock, hanging out abruptly over the water. Our party were intensely animated with the scene, and came on shore at Tremont in high spirits.*

They lodged at the Mount Desert House in Somesville and stayed for more than a month, roving about the entire island, enjoying "chemically perfect" air. Before they left the island, Tracy and Church threw a raucous dinner party for eighty people—the kind of party that left chandeliers in relics and sent guests stumbling home at 2:00 a.m.

The event was still being talked about two years later, when a *New York Daily Times* writer, Elizabeth B. Stoddard, heard about it. The writer intended her article to be a guide to future travelers. In describing the delicious air, effortless walking, and stunning scenery, Stoddard was not only advertising Acadia to potential visitors, but to potential hosts. "In time, their keepers will provide good mattresses, long thick towels, a convenient washstand apparatus, including large wash bowls, water pails, and last, but not least, bread made with leaven."

Despite their complaints, the artists liked Acadia's rough-around-the-edges appeal. As Bar Harbor historian Richard Hale noted in *The Story of Bar Harbor*, "They liked to have their meals at hours that fitted a farmer, not them; they liked to sleep in hot attics—or, at least, to tell about it later on. And they liked to be treated as slightly mad human beings who were alright as long as one left them alone. Because it was such a happy life, the artists spoke of Mount Desert as a heavenly spot in which to rest and enjoy oneself."

While the artists are credited with creating a tourism industry in Acadia, they worked together with scientists and writers to advertise the place. As they shared information, advanced their careers, and satisfied their own desires for beauty, the first tourists made others want to come to the place they had read about and seen.

In 1858 the *New York Tribune* published an account of a cruise from Boston to Mount Desert by Washington correspondent Robert Carter (later published as a book). Sailing aboard the cod-fishing schooner *Helen of Swampscott*, Carter and Smithsonian ichthyology professor and expert crab-catcher William Stimpson surveyed marine organisms along the way. Also aboard were Francis Underwood of the *Atlantic Monthly* and artist Henry Ware.

As they left Eggemoggin Reach, "the peaks of Mount Desert came gradually into view, at first misty and blue, then green and wooded, until, as we advanced, still loftier summits showed themselves in grim and stony desolation." They landed at Bass Harbor and traveled to Southwest Harbor, Bar Harbor, Otter Creek, Great Head, and Schooner Head.

Carter had more advice for would-be hosts: "Of late years, Mount Desert has become a favorite resort for artists and for sea-side summer loungers. But it needs the hand of cultivated taste for the full development of its matchless natural beauties, which, at present, are to a great degree hidden by the monotonous covering of an American forest of the secondary growth."

Expecting the "forest primeval," Carter was disappointed by the "judicious clearing" of "lovely glades and charming, yet stately groves" that should have been surrounding the mountains. He thought the landscape demanded the high genius of a landscape gardener who could create "a picturesque and proper contrast of light and shade, of rural grace and of wild and stern grandeur."

Carter also acknowledged the artists who had come before him: "It is difficult to conceive of any finer combination of land and water than this view, which has been admirably painted by Charles Dix."

Dix was among the artists who followed Cole, Church, and Fitz Henry Lane, a distinguished group that also included John Kensett, Regis Giroux, Albert Bierstadt, and William Stanley Haseltine. Haseltine also was motivated by science, his "rock portraits" displaying a fidelity to nature. Isle au Haut and Schoodic received the attention of artists, but much less so than Mount Desert.

The majority of images featured ocean scenes, most with shoreline rocks and cliffs. Many had sailboats; some had mountains. People were present, most often overwhelmed by scenery. A few showed a hardy sailor hauling some piece of wreckage ashore. Landscape as salvation: The story did not change.

By the middle of the nineteenth century, photographs joined paintings, drawings, and written accounts of Acadia. Photography reflected a shift in visitor trends and the tourism industry, away from pure wilderness toward a more cosmopolitan experience. The earliest landscape photograph of the island, in 1855, showed the new Agamont House hotel in Bar Harbor.

Photography became important to tourism promotion with the completion of a comprehensive network of rail lines after the Civil War. Trains and steamboats made Maine accessible from Philadelphia, New York, and Boston.

John Heywood arrived to make the first series of stereo views of Mount Desert Island, followed closely by fellow Boston photographer Edward Allen. Their photographs focused on prominent coastal and

PICTURESQUE AMERICA.

Castle Head, Mount Desert.

ON THE COAST OF MAINE.

WITH ILLUSTRATIONS BY HARRY FENN.

THE island of Mount Desert, on the coast of Maine, unites a striking group of picturesque features. It is surrounded by seas, crowned with mountains, and embosomed
with lakes. Its shores are bold and rocky cliffs, upon which the breakers for countless centuries have wrought their ceaseless attrition. It affords the only instance along our Atlantic
coast where mountains stand in close neighborhood to the sea; here in one picture are

The opening page of William Cullen Bryant's *Picturesque America*, 1872.

landscape features of the island, scenes of farming, fishing, lumbering, and shipbuilding, and the early hotels and boardinghouses.

Five of Edward Allen's images illustrated Clara Barnes Martin's 1874 *Mount Desert, on the Coast of Maine*, the 115-page book published by Short & Harmon of Portland. The book had evolved from Martin's original, 36-page pamphlet published in 1867. Martin's father edited the *Portland Advertiser*, she contributed to the literary columns of the *New York Post* and *The Nation*. Oliver Wendell Holmes was a family friend.

To Martin, Mount Desert culminated the wonder of the Maine coast; the rest of the East Coast was "monotonous." The Isle of Shoals, Wachusett, Nahant, Mount Monadnock, Newport, and the Catskills could all be found in one location at Acadia. Martin described the geology, history, scenic views, forests, coastal chasms, and caves, along with the fish that could be caught in the ponds, and quoted poems by Whittier and Browning.

She covered the "peculiar topography" at length, as tourists wanted to know the names of mountains and ponds and identify them by their outlines, best seen while sailing between Bar and Southwest Harbors. She told which places were most popular and worth visiting—or not, such as Sargent Mountain Pond, "a small lake of much reputation" but by one account not very attractive. She wrote not just where to go and how, but when: The drive from Bar Harbor to Otter Creek was "pleasantest in the afternoon when the western shadows are long." She noted the commonality of Indian relics, but did not mention the population of Wabanaki then living in the region.

Martin expected that by this time, readers may have already heard or read about Mount Desert. The island's many harbors were "well known." The top of Green (Cadillac) Mountain had "long been visited by tourists." She also was sure to identify scenes painted by artists, such as Great Head, and she herself tried (in vain) to sketch a sunset. Mount Desert Rock appeared in both the excerpt from Whittier's poem and Martin's recollection of a twilight scene. She warned that the trip to see it, however, was "too long and too rough for many."

A year after Martin's first edition, Benjamin F. DeCosta published *Scenes in the Isle of Mount Desert, Coast of Maine*, with photographs by John Heywood. In addition to the typical coast and summit views, Heywood photographed men lounging in fields overlooking the sea or standing in the grass.

DeCosta encouraged American readers to look no farther than their own backyard for natural beauty: "We have every variety of mountain and coast scenery, equal, if not superior, to that of foreign countries, almost within sight of all of our doors." He, too, had to compare the views to more familiar scenes like the Delaware Water Gap and the Hudson River, and to mention Mount Desert Rock, as if the beacon was already a well-known landmark. Later editions, retitled *Rambles in Mount Desert*, had fewer images.

Despite the growing tourist towns, Acadia was still for adventurers primarily in search of natural scenery and wonder in 1872, when William Cullen Bryant's *Picturesque America* showed Harry Fenn's sketch of Acadia on the very first plate, as viewed from the water. The book opens with "On the Coast of Maine" by Oliver Bell Bunce:

> *Here in one picture are beetling cliffs with the roar of restless breakers, far stretches of bay dotted with green islands, placid mountain-lakes mirroring the mountain-precipices that tower above them, rugged gorges clothed with primitive forests, and sheltered coves where the sea-waves ripple on the shelly beach. Upon the shores are masses of cyclopean rocks heaped one upon another in titanic disorder, and strange caverns of marvellous beauty; on the mountains are frightful precipices, wonderful prospects of far-extending sea, and mazes of land and water, and magnificent forests of fir and spruce. It is a union of all these supreme fascinations of scenery, such as Nature, munificent as she is, rarely affords.*

Consisting of two leather-bound volumes totaling over one thousand pages, *Picturesque America* presented places considered to be "characteristic" of America. Published by Bryant to show Americans they had "a variety of scenery which no other country can boast of, the wildest and noblest scenery in the world . . . where the spectator, surprised at this vastness, finds himself overpowered with a sense of sublimity," it was a showcase for landscape artists to show Americans new places. *Picturesque America* was also a travel guide, instructing readers on travel itineraries ("the steamer from Portland approaches the island at noonday"), where to go ("proceed first to the Ovens"), and what to see and do when they got there ("picnic in the caves . . . pluck the wild-roses, and roam up and down the beach in search of the strange creatures of the sea").

The same year, *Harper's New Monthly Magazine* featured a lengthy article on Mount Desert. The opening page has a print of "Cave of the Sea, Schooner Head":

A beautiful picture was before us. Seaward and to the southeast the steel-blue waters, roughened here and there by the wind, which came in gentle flaws, spread out to the far-off horizon, where the clouds, with shadows of pearl-gray, and the tops in sunlight tinged with vermillion and gold, seemed dipping into the sea. A league away, and right before us, every instant a white wave would leap into the air, and then, with irregular, uneven motion, but swiftly, it would run in toward us and toward a bleak line of beach and rocky shore . . . More loftily, and in more decided forms, these might mountains, some thirteen peaks in all, rise out of the clear waters, their graceful outlines sweeping across the blue sky, their summits bare, hard, and unyielding, and with the strong flood of vertical sunlight which now pours down upon them, they have a burnished, brazen look. The lines of shadows, too, made by deep ravines or wide valleys, are sharp and hard, lacking the softening grace which the presence of foliage lends, but all the contours are of the simple, sweeping, but most impressive mountain forms. They are not half the height of the White Mountains, yet are far more beautiful, for they are not cut up into several dumpy peaks, and broken in their descent, but from their highest summit undulate gracefully downward into the sea.

The *Harper's* story described the type of people who would visit Mount Desert, and in so doing preselected tourists with an affinity for the rustic. People who would overlook bad food, uncomfortable beds, and rude hosts to partake in the "bounteous feast which nature spreads before

HARPER'S
NEW MONTHLY MAGAZINE.

No. CCLXVII.—AUGUST, 1872.—Vol. XLV.

MOUNT DESERT.

CAVE OF THE SEA, SCHOONER HEAD.

SINCE early morning we have been gliding swiftly over the quiet waters which encircle the thousands of islands along the coast of Maine.

During the night, when sleeping, and while journeying from Portland to Rockland, a fog stole in upon us from the ocean. We are again upon our way, and now the sharp prow of our goodly sized steamer seems to cut its way into the gray wall which appears to be impenetrable, but which, however quickly we may move along, is always before us, by our side, and closes up immediately behind us.

In the midst of this intense fog, when you can hardly recognize your best friend half the length of the steamer, you would suppose the pilot at the wheel would move with hesitation; but it is no extravagance of speech to say that he knows every inch of the way.

Very often the steamer turns to the right and the left, with no apparent obstruction in its path, but never does it slacken speed. Standing at the bow of the boat, the ear of inexperience even detects at times the presence of land by the sound of the thumping paddle-wheels returning in sullen echoes from the rocky cliffs, whose wave-washed base quickly appears to view, almost within reach of hand, and as quickly vanishes from sight behind the gray veil of fog.

The morning by this time has advanced, and we are conscious that the all-pervading atmosphere of gray has become gradually, and by imperceptible degrees, of a delicate cream-white. It is an exquisite ethereal substance, the despair of the artist to paint, beyond description; for while you are gazing, for an instant a gentle breeze fans your cheek, and then, by one of nature's magical trans-

them." People who wore hiking boots and flannel. "There is a vigorous, sensible, healthy feeling in all that they do, and not a bit of that over-dressed, pretentious, nonsensical, unhealthy sentimentality which may be found at other places." The author continued, "In all my wanderings I remember no place where the lover of the beautiful, the romantic, and the more sublime elements of nature will find so much that will fascinate and captivate him as here."

The undeniable power of images helped launch the national park movement, when the strange beauty captured in Thomas Moran's watercolor sketches and oils, and William Jackson's photographs, persuaded the US Congress to pass the bill creating Yellowstone, America's first national park.

Images also helped to market parks to the masses. The number of people visiting Bar Harbor had doubled and then doubled again. Some two dozen hotels had been constructed on Mount Desert Island, and Bar Harbor was well on its way to becoming a major tourist attraction in itself. Boston's J. R. Osgood & Company's booklet *Mt. Desert Portrayed in Crayon and Quill* captured the social side of summer life in Bar Harbor: gatherings on porches and waterfronts, at the post office, or on jolting buckboard rides.

After a hotel was constructed on the top of Green (Cadillac) Mountain, the proprietors had to advertise it. Broadsheets advised tourists, "You have not seen Mt. Desert until you have viewed it from the summit of Green Mountain." The most extensive and beautiful view along the Atlantic coast could be reached by an easy drive up the carriage toll road along the north slope.

Beginning in 1883 tourists could ride a cog railway to the summit, where thousands of people visited each year. In *Summer Days Down East*, Moses Sweetser observed the change. No longer a paradise of the unconventional, where comfortably clad summer-idlers unbent their yearlong city formalisms and indulged in "rural amusements," Mount Desert Island had become home to a "cottage aristocracy" of seasonal residents

"Here Florence, deftly tripping o'er the strand, oft begged for Reginald's supporting hand" read the caption for this scene from J.R. Osgood & Co.'s tourist booklet, *Mt. Desert in 1873, Portrayed in Crayon & Quill.*
COURTESY OF SPECIAL COLLECTIONS, RAYMOND H. FOGLER LIBRARY, UNIVERSITY OF MAINE, ORONO, MAINE

and great hotels that restricted the freedom of short-term vacationers and introduced an element of "stately decorum of Newport and Nahant."

Booklets of Acadia images, printed by the Albertype Company of New York (*Scenery of Mount Desert*) and Forbes Company of Boston (*Mount Desert Views*), served as souvenirs, so tourists could show their friends and family at home the places they had been.

As hotel life and extravagance prospered in Bar Harbor, people heard equally about the social life of the "Fish Pond" at Rodick's hotel as they did about the Ovens, Eagle Lake, or the summit of Green (Cadillac) Mountain. "Bar Harbor" had become "synonymous with merry courtships and happy, irresponsible days," wrote historian George Street. Many lamented the passing of the "rusticator" period, when people came

The romance of Bar Harbor, in *Bar Harbor Days*, 1887. H. FENN/GOOGLE BOOKS

Boating scenes from Lapham's guide, *Bar Harbor and Mount Desert Island*, 1886. ARCHIVE.ORG

primarily for the scenery. Instead, Acadia had joined the extensive "plea-sure periphery" for the metropolitan upper classes that stretched from Cape May to Campobello and St. Andrews.

William Berry Lapham dedicated much of his book, *Bar Harbor and Mount Desert Island (with Pen and Pencil)* to the rapid growth of Bar Harbor. The first illustration shows the busy village from offshore, with a crowd of sailboats in between: "The island is being surrounded by a cordon of invaders, and the time will come when all the land bordering on or near the sea, will be cut up into houselots for their use."

Cover of Lapham's guide, *Bar Harbor and Mount Desert Island*, 1886. ARCHIVE.ORG

The crowds at Bar Harbor drove some New York and Philadelphia families to seek summer property farther afield, founding the Grindstone Neck summer colony at Schoodic. Ernest Bowditch of Boston began building a summer resort on Isle au Haut.

By the early 1900s, images of hotels and summer mansions ("cottages"), steamships, and railroads had supplanted the scenic views of Acadia. The emphasis on tourism fit the mission of the National Park Service, which upon its creation in 1916 inherited a system of parks designed to enhance public enjoyment. To avoid competing directly with the Forest Service, the new agency emphasized recreation and tourism, facilitated by railroads at first and later by automobiles.

As national park historian Richard Sellars noted, accommodating the "use and enjoyment" of nature by the public fostered a business-oriented approach to parks that emphasized the number of miles of roads and

Bar Harbor view from Chisolm's *Souvenir of Bar Harbor.* COURTESY OF SPECIAL COLLECTIONS, RAYMOND H. FOGLER LIBRARY, UNIVERSITY OF MAINE, ORONO, MAINE

trails, how many hotel rooms and campsites were available, and trends in visitor use. Robert Sterling Yard, writing in the *Nation's Business*, argued that more than an aesthetic luxury, scenery had commercial value, and the parks needed some promotion. America had to move beyond "just conserving" them to developing them, with roads and trails, hotels and campgrounds.

Government and corporate brochures from the first half of the twentieth century emphasized accessibility and a shift toward auto travel. A 1929 Bar Harbor brochure by Sherman Publishing Company with photos

Lafayette [Acadia] National Park guidebook, 1923.
ACADIA NATIONAL PARK

by Herbert Gleason confirmed that "nowhere in the world is there such a wonderland of sea, cliff, lake and forest as nature has lavished on this great Maine Coast Resort," but "no vacation trip to Maine can be complete without a visit to Bar Harbor, America's most distinguished resort." Golf, motoring, yachting, and horseback riding were the first activities described. Government-issue pamphlets touted the new Cadillac Mountain summit road.

In the 1930s artist Edgar Hegh resided at the Civilian Conservation Corps' McFarland Camp. He documented the life and work of the CCC, as well as the landscape of the park, in paintings and sketches.

The advertising worked. The number of people visiting Acadia increased from 22,000 in 1887 to 50,000 in 1917 to 64,000 in 1919 to more than 400,000 in the early 1940s. The ever-increasing popularity of Mount Desert Island motivated some artists to find their way to Schoodic in the 1940s, including photographers Ansel Adams and Bernice Abbott and Maine painter Marsden Hartley.

After World War II, and despite work by the Civilian Conservation Corps, Acadia and other national parks were deteriorating, with newspaper and magazine articles highlighting the trashy conditions of many. One-fifth of Americans couldn't identify a single national park; the rest preferred to experience their parks from behind the wheel. Visitors complained of overcrowding and lack of sightseeing guides, maps, and other information (by one estimate, twenty-two million pieces of literature were needed). Concerned, Acadia supporter John D. Rockefeller Jr. was among those who pressed President Eisenhower to provide more funding for park management and maintenance.

Reorganization of the Interior Department prompted a comprehensive program to launch the national parks into the modern era. Termed "Mission 66" for the anticipated fiftieth anniversary of the National Park Service in 1966, and funded with a decade of congressional money, the program planned 25,000 campsites, 2,000 miles of new roads, 1,500 miles of new trails, 300 sewer systems, 96 campfire circles and amphitheaters, and 76 ranger stations.

Acadia National Park guidebook, 1938.
ACADIA NATIONAL PARK

Walt Disney reinforced the initiative with a film, *Adventure in the National Parks*. Circulation of *Our Heritage*, a promotional booklet, reminded Americans, and their congressional representatives, that "the National Park System is a national resource—natural, historical, cultural. Like other resources, it has meaning and value only when converted into products useful to man. The problem is simply this: the National Parks are neither equipped nor staffed to protect their irreplaceable features, nor to take care of the increasing millions of visitors."

Acadia National Park guidebook, 1940.
ACADIA NATIONAL PARK

With the emergence of the environmental movement, more people than ever wanted to witness the American outdoors, but their experience was lessened by "masses of people who crowd to the same spot to see the same view at the same time—and many visitors leave with curiosity unsatisfied, enjoyment and appreciate incomplete—all because the National Park Service does not have the facilities nor the personnel to help the visitors know and comprehend what it is they see."

Thanks to Bar Harbor and other towns, Acadia did not have the lodging problem of the more remote western parks, where Mission 66 crews addressed camping and housing. Mission 66 plans included 109 visitor centers designed to "elevate the parks to modern standards of comfort and efficiency while conserving natural resources." Mission 66 plans called for efficient, centralized spaces where visitors could circulate easily, locate essential services, and learn the park's "story." Acadia's headquarters building, designed in the modernist style by architects Ehrman Mitchell and Romaldo Giurgola, was never built. At other parks, Mission 66 structures were not received well by an environmentalist and nostalgic public.

Around the time that Mission 66 was playing out on Mount Desert Island, the owner of the mail boat ferry to Isle au Haut married a motel owner from Stonington. The enterprising couple became much more active in promoting tourism, advertising the Isle au Haut unit of Acadia widely throughout the Northeast and delivering a growing number of tourists unaccompanied to the town dock. The new arrivals alarmed the locals, prompting some to purchase the mail boat and discontinue all advertising. They began a community planning effort which envisioned a modest increase in year-round population and a traditional resource-based economy independent of tourism.

But the word was out.

Despite more active management at Isle au Haut, the National Park Service did not prepare visitors for what they would encounter on the small island. Dropped off at the town landing, tourists seemed to think the whole island was their playground. They camped and picnicked in people's yards, wandered awestruck and aimless through town. In response, summer people and year-rounders began talking about shared concerns and working together with the Park Service.

Unlike Mount Desert, on Isle au Haut the year-round villages remained separate and distinct from the park, with limited interaction between the two populations by design. Advertisement, too, was kept to a minimum, and the community maintained its resistance to promotion, leaving Isle au Haut to 1 percent of Acadia visitors who wanted to be away from the fray and didn't succumb to marketing ploys.

By the twenty-first century, the overwhelming number of images and competition for visitor attention had both diluted and distributed the experience for visitors—more than two million every year since 1964.

Acadia consistently ranked among the top ten most-visited national parks in the United States. Mount Desert Rock, with its shipwrecks and fog, lost its allure to urban audiences, but the other images that first created destination Acadia remained as salient as ever.

Brochures, guidebooks, magazines, and websites featured the same attractions: the summit of Cadillac, the eastern cliffs of Mount Desert, Sand Beach, Bar Harbor, Jordan Pond House, the big breaking waves of Schoodic Point. All great things to see and do, but tourists could mar the Acadia experience not only for residents, certainly, but also for other tourists. If Doughty, Cole, Church, Martin, DeCosta, and the rest were alive today, they might have chosen to paint Acadia in winter, the woods heavy with snow, the ponds frozen solid, lone fishing vessels amid the eiders in the frigid sea, and the mountains empty of people—and silent.

Arrival

How People Came to Acadia

The approach to Mount Desert by sea is magnificent. The island is a mass of mountains crowded together, and seemingly rising from the water. As you draw near, they resolve themselves into thirteen distinct peaks, the highest of which is about two thousand feet above the neighboring ocean. It is difficult to conceive of any finer combination of land and water than this view.

—Robert Carter, *A Summer Cruise on the Coast of New England*

They had been traveling so long, surrounded by water, only the *petrels and the porpoise to keep them company. And then, in the distance, a blue shadow of a hill. As they got closer, the hill begat other hills, a silhouette of mountain and valley filling the horizon between the gray-blue water and the white-blue sky. Racing the dazzling sunlight on the waves, their bow scattering seabirds, they steered toward the land. As they got closer, they could see bare rock on the tops of the hills, and craggy cliffs strewn with trees. Shadows on the forested slopes suggested a deep and varied topography. How could they not want to approach such a place?*

An imagined experience of early travelers to Acadia, who came by water. The Wabanaki paddled and sailed to Pemetic, Schoodic, and Isle au Haut in all seasons, using the ingenious, strong, and lightweight birch bark canoe, shallops procured from visiting European fishermen and explorers, and possibly dugout canoes. They weaved their way through lakes and rivers, portaging from one watershed to the next, or else traveled through the regional archipelago and the open sea.

Europeans, too, came by boat. Portuguese, Italian, and French explorers found the waters filled with fish and the forests thick with good trees. Perhaps because they heard the Native people call the place *ekati, quoddy,* or perhaps from the beauty and abundance they observed, they named the place *Arkadia, L'Acadie,* lush wooded mountain wilderness, a place to live in peace and harmony with nature. Unaware of the impossibility of their idyllic vision, they believed the new territory was God's reward for a new beginning. Many could not go home; others would not. They settled.

More came from Gloucester and Cape Cod, Scotland and England. In 1761 Abraham Somes established a homestead near the head of the saltwater sound. Somes was a cooper, a maker of barrels, and the sheltered harbor had running water and plenty of hardwood. He returned to Gloucester the next year for his family, bringing them up in Chebacco boats, small two-masted sailing vessels used for fishing close to shore (named after Chebacco Parish of Ipswich, Massachusetts, where many were built). Within two years, nine immigrants had established households on Mount Desert. The Barters arrived on Isle au Haut around 1788, Thomas Frazer established a home at Schoodic, and they were followed by more settlers seeking to take advantage of the emerging fishing industry.

All of the residents traveled around and between islands with boats, placing early settlements near the shore for easy access. Those on Mount Desert Island reached the mainland to the north by fording the narrow channel and mudflats at low tide or, after 1770, catching a small private ferry.

As George Street noted in his history of Mount Desert Island, "The new free lands were an irresistible bait, the harbors were unequaled, the great woods promised inexhaustible supplies of timber, the waters teemed with fish, and the rushing streams gave power for grist and lumber mills."

Horse-drawn stagecoaches and carriages—as well as people on foot—traveled the roads. Mount Desert Island's first road, constructed in

The bridge from Trenton to Mount Desert Island, ca. 1920. JESUP MEMORIAL LIBRARY

1765, stretched from Somesville to Southwest Harbor, by way of Beech Hill. Another road ran along the shore of Northeast Harbor. Other roads connected farms and logging camps with ports on the coast. Schooner Head Road, Breakneck Road, and parts of Route 233 and Route 3 were in place by 1835. Two years later, the Mount Desert Bridge Corporation built a wooden toll drawbridge across the Mount Desert Narrows to Trenton on the mainland.

On Isle au Haut, road networks were limited to the island's perimeter, used mostly by "summer people" without ready access to boats. By 1860, four thousand people resided in Acadia, all around Mount Desert, along the thoroughfare of Isle au Haut, and Schoodic's Winter Harbor, in addition to the Wabanaki who maintained their ancestral presence.

Those who did not have their own boats still came by water. Steam-powered passenger ships had been running between Boston and Penobscot Bay since the 1820s. Steamship service came to Southwest Harbor from Rockland (via the *Rockland*) in the 1850s and from Machiasport (via the *City of Richmond*) in the 1860s. Regular service to Bar Harbor began in 1868, with construction of a wharf and arrival of the 246-foot *Lewiston*. The Bar Harbor wharf was subsequently purchased and expanded by the Eastern Railroad Company. In 1880 at least six ferries made more trips carrying visitors and summer residents (and their horses) to Acadia, including the nimble, 162-foot *Mount Desert*, built specifically for travel to the region. Smaller ferries and steamboats joined the fleet.

As their vessels approached Acadia, passengers got the same sense as early navigators. Travel writer Charles Howard Shinn reported on the journey in the *Overland Monthly*, "Suddenly new groups of isles in the blue sea, and beyond them, intensely purple, and far more rounded and great and satisfying than one had imagined, the heights of Mount Desert's continent-like island fill the horizon."

Appalled at the living conditions of some local families (and lack of agriculture), Portlander Clara Barnes Martin believed that the people

Steamship *Mount Desert* leaving Southwest Harbor, ca. 1900. W. H. BALLARD/MOUNT DESERT ISLAND HISTORICAL SOCIETY

of Mount Desert would benefit from "a better acquaintance with the rest of the world." But such advancement would not come so long as an expensive stage-ride, or the uncertain dependence of sailing ships, were their only links with outside life. To Martin, the steamboat ferries were a great improvement.

Not until later in the nineteenth century did people arrive by water by choice, as sailing for pleasure became popular among those who could afford it.

May, 1871: Charles W. Eliot had been president of Harvard barely two years, and a widower just as long. He needed a break, for himself and his two young sons, a "thorough vacation" in the open air, as he wrote to a friend.

He bought *Jessie*, a thirty-three-foot sloop, and began planning a sailing and camping trip to Maine, "down Mount Desert way." Described as "a very pretty boat and tolerably fast," *Jessie* made a few warm-up excursions around Boston Harbor and raced with the Dorchester Yacht Club

Mount Desert Island steamship *J.T. Morse*. W.H. BALLARD/MOUNT DESERT ISLAND HISTORICAL SOCIETY

before leaving for Maine in July. Captained by Charles W. Eliot (with assistance from a hired sailor) and crewed by his brother-in-law Charles Eliot Guild, nephew Robert Wheaton Guild, and Arthur C. Kelley of Neponset, the boat was jammed full of camping gear, leaving little room for the passengers in the four berths below.

They reached Portland in a day, then went on to anchorages in Herring Gut and Deer Island Thoroughfare. As they made Bass Harbor Light, the fog cleared away. They passed Long Ledge and Great Cranberry and sailed into Southwest Harbor, where they anchored before dusk.

It was the first of many seasons which would instill in Charles W. Eliot, and especially his sons Charles and Samuel, a sense of place and understanding that would have a lasting impact on the Mount Desert region and beyond. Young Charles Eliot would lead the first natural history surveys of the island as "captain" of the Champlain Society in the 1880s. And when he founded The Trustees of Reservations in Massachusetts in 1891, Charles Eliot created the land trust model that would be used to protect Acadia's diverse landscapes and many other places around the world.

The log of the Eliots' 1871 cruise and subsequent ones, preserved by the Mount Desert Island Historical Society, describe what sailing was like in those early years.

On Saturday, July 15, *Jessie* sailed over to Bar Harbor to pick up the boys, Charles, eleven, and Sam, eight, and their attending nursemaid. The following day they were joined by their cousin Mary, aunt Fan, and uncle Reverend Henry Wilder Foote, minister to King's Chapel in Boston.

They spent the summer tasting the salt of coastal life, picnicking in island fields, chasing butterflies through the sea-washed air, and combing woods and wrack lines for treasures. According to Charles W. Eliot's biographer, Henry James, a sense of novelty and excitement was part of the fun. "Once away on these holidays, Harvard and his ordinary cares seemed to drop out of Eliot's mind. The sea, the wind, the day and its small adventures, the procuring of supplies, the sailing of the boat absorbed him completely," wrote James.

Back in Cambridge that fall, Charles W. Eliot knew he would return to Calf Island. The thought of another summer on the Maine coast made bearable the prospect of another year managing Harvard. He immediately made plans to sell *Jessie*. He needed a vessel that was better suited to extended cruising with friends and family.

There were no professional yacht designers at the time, as "yachting" itself was relatively new, having become more popular after the Civil War. By the late 1860s, fifty large yachts sailed about Boston Harbor, where only a handful had been a decade earlier. Boston emerged alongside New York as a center of American yachting. Around Boston the anchorages were deeper and the boats more likely to be sailed in exposed waters, so they tended to be deeper-draft keelboats. Still, most yachts were designed by their owners or were spin-offs of merchant and fishing ships.

For example, Robert Carter's 1858 cruise, chronicled in the *New York Tribune*, used a fishing schooner; likewise, in 1865 a retrofitted schooner carried a party of nineteen (including six female) Quakers and crew of six from Long Island to "the place of which everyone seemed to be speaking." According to the published account of their trip, *The Cruise of the Forest Home*,

> *We now shaped our course direct to Mount Desert, the ultima thule of our anticipations. We could see, far over the intervening land and water, the elevated peaks of its thirteen great mountains, which in that pure atmosphere loomed grandly against the sky . . . As we approached Mount Desert the breeze gradually died out; and when, just as the sun was setting, we reached the mouth of South West Harbor, scarcely a breath of air ruffled the surface of the long ocean rollers which were dashing themselves to foam on the great ledge of rock which forms a natural breakwater at the entrance. The wind's dying breath scarce sufficed to fill our idle canvas; but the advancing tide drifted us slowly and noiselessly onward, and amid the solemn stillness of the deepening twilight we entered the beautiful Bay. Our party were congregated at the bow of the vessel, drinking in with insatiable delight the varied and ever to be remembered beauties of that evening view.*

They dropped anchor at Southwest Harbor off Deacon Clark's Island House hotel; the ladies gathered on the deck in the moonlight, singing. The next day they took the advice of a local hotel owner "that one of the finest and most extended views which the island afforded could be obtained from the summit of Dog [St. Sauveur] Mountain," and set off accordingly. The following day they went on a "grand fishing excursion" for cod, haddock, and pollock. They visited Otter Creek and Spouting Horn, Devil's Oven (Anemone Cave), and Thunder Hole.

Charles W. Eliot custom-designed a yacht for cruising the New England coast. Built by Albertson Brothers of Philadelphia and finished at Foster's boatyard in East Boston, the forty-three-and-a-half-foot sloop *Sunshine* had a cabin tall enough to accommodate standing adults and room enough for six. James called it "one of the first American yachts designed specifically for cruising along the New England coast."

The Eliots returned to Calf Island in 1872 and again from 1874 to 1879. Charles W. Eliot had learned to sail at a young age in the waters around the rugged shores of Nahant, where his father had built a summer home, and he had camped in college, while on summer "walking-journeys"

The Eliot family yacht, *Sunshine*, at anchor near High Head, 1881. M. P. SLADE/
MOUNT DESERT ISLAND HISTORICAL SOCIETY

and scientific excursions along the Atlantic coast with professors and fellow students. He wanted the same for his sons.

With the Coast Survey's *Atlantic Coast Pilot* as a guide, and the historic voyages of Samuel de Champlain as inspiration, the Eliots came to know the harbors, shoals, islands, and beaches of the Maine coast. Young Charles and Sam learned that health and happiness were within easy reach in the Acadian summer.

Travel at the time was still fairly rustic, and that was the idea.

Later in the nineteenth century, people took to the water in pleasure craft and racing boats. People from Boston and Baltimore, Portland and Philadelphia, Charleston and Chicago, sailed about Mount Desert Island in swift catamarans and graceful yachts.

Sailing was a natural extension of an increasing desire to get out of the crowded city, and one that was faster and more calming than a bumpy stagecoach ride or crowded steamship, which is how most visitors arrived at Acadia at the time.

———

Things changed in 1884, with construction of Maine Central Railroad's tracks to the coast at Hancock. Visitors could arrive via train and a short ferry ride from Hancock Point. Seven days a week, seven trains a day rolled across the Penobscot River, through the boulder fields of the Dedham hills to the landing at Mount Desert Ferry (McNeil Point), where they transferred to a steamship ferry for a final eight-mile leg across Frenchman Bay to Mount Desert.

The Maine Shore Line daily excursion train, too crowded and slow for some, created demand for a first-class alternative with a limited number of stops, new and more efficient technology, and elegant, lightweight Pullman cars. The Bar Harbor Express, the fastest express train in the United States at its inception in 1887, was the transportation of choice for wealthy families traveling to Mount Desert Island from Boston, New York, and Philadelphia, up until the time of World War I. With ferries being put to military service, the gilded age of Acadia travel ended.

People had been driving around the mainland since the turn of the century, but transportation did not shift as quickly on Mount Desert

Island. Most of the wealthy summer residents resisted cars, fearing the transformation of their carefully developed seasonal home. Year-round residents wanted cars and roads, but they lacked the influence to prevent a 1909 law prohibiting vehicles from Mount Desert Island. Auto advocates soon prevailed. With the exception of Norway Drive, Breakneck Drive, and Ocean Drive, all of Eden's roads opened to the automobile by 1915.

Among those who welcomed (or at least didn't fight) automobiles, John D. Rockefeller Jr. had been building a network of carriage roads on and around his Seal Harbor estate. He learned the art from his father, Standard Oil magnate John D. Rockefeller Sr., who engineered roads and bridges on his country estates. Believing a separate "motor road" system would preserve the rest of the island for pedestrians and carriages, Rockefeller Jr. sponsored—and supervised—much of the early road construction in Acadia. Landscape gardening theory influenced the design of the roads, which carried the rider or the walker through a sequence of selected landscape "events." Rockefeller used the same approach in laying out motor roads.

A charge from National Park Service director Stephen Mather to all parks to develop roads and trails added further motivation to Rockefeller's financial support. At the time, Acadia National Park centered around Mount Desert's eastern summits, an area difficult to access by horse or automobile.

Under the direction of Rockefeller and Acadia superintendent George Dorr, engineers Paul Simpson and Walters Hill completed the first section of automobile road within the park in July 1924. The 4,300 feet of road from Eagle Lake Road (Route 233) to the intersection with (the proposed) Cadillac Mountain Road set a benchmark for quality within the national parks.

Summer residents hated it. Fearing loud, littering crowds along a multiplying road network, they wrote letters to persuade the secretary of the interior to abandon the project. But roads had broad support among the year-round residents, Maine's congressional delegation, and a few influential seasonal residents such as Rockefeller and Charles W. Eliot. Construction continued.

John D. Rockefeller, Jr. COURTESY OF ROCKEFELLER ARCHIVE CENTER

The next section, open from 7:00 a.m. to 9:00 p.m., with a speed limit of eighteen miles per hour, went to Jordan Pond. The asphalt pavement incorporated granite from a quarry near Bubble Pond, making the road blend into the landscape. In 1926 the Federal Highway Administration and the National Park Service began cooperating on the design, construction, and rehabilitation of roads within national parks. Cadillac Mountain Road was among the first to be built under this new agreement, in 1933.

The views from Cadillac had prompted travel by foot, cart, and carriage to the summit since US Coast Survey crews constructed a rough path up the north ridge of the mountain in the 1850s. Rockefeller believed it a logical place for an automobile road. He worked on the alignment of the road and made sure the banks and edges were treated to the standards of his other roads and carriage roads.

Cadillac Mountain Road was described as an amazing example of construction on mountainous terrain. A maximum grade of 7 percent required that the road ascend uphill for its entire length. Spiral transition curves, an adaptation from the techniques of the railroad industry, created a smoother, flowing transition between straight and curved sections.

Meanwhile, Rockefeller improved the drive along the ocean on the eastern shore of Mount Desert Island, a town road since the 1890s, as part of a "demonstration project." His road vision expanded, and Rockefeller brought in the experts: the Olmsted Brothers firm of Brookline, Massachusetts.

When news broke of the four-million-dollar plan, summer residents again protested, while year-round locals supported the effort to "civilize" the island.

While they waited for the controversy to resolve, the Olmsteds, sons of Frederick Law Olmsted, worked on Rockefeller's own private roads at Stanley Brook (the same firm had worked on Rockefeller's family estate in the Pocantico Hills of New York). Assisted by crews of laborers, the landscape architects measured each curve and straightaway, avoiding certain trees while pruning away other vegetation.

With the rest of the road plan finally approved in 1933, construction at Stanley Brook and Otter Cliffs began, but completion of this section required relocating the naval radio station at Otter Cliffs. Dorr had the idea to move the naval station to the new unit of the park at Schoodic Point. Rockefeller enthusiastically agreed. He constructed six buildings at the new base, while Civilian Conservation Corps crews moved the station to Schoodic Point.

As part of the New Deal, Congress provided more money for park roads and other development, and the CCC constructed a new four-mile road along old carriage tracks at Schoodic and built a parking lot to view the surf at the point. The CCC camped at McFarland Hill and Southwest Harbor on Mount Desert, where they fabricated road-related gates, curbing, fences, and signs and restored roadside vegetation.

A combination of private and public sources funded construction of the remainder of the Park Loop Road (Day Mountain, Paradise Hill to Hulls Cove, Champlain Mountain section). Work paused during World War II, then Mission 66 funding helped complete the loop in 1958—just in time, as the train stopped running in 1960. Mission 66, named for its intended completion date in 1966, was the federal government's billion-dollar plan to improve park facilities, increase staffing, and enhance tourism in the national parks.

The road moved people through the landscape, at times in tunnels of foliage, at other times offering vistas of mountain and lake. Cars slipped through valleys and around hills, the asphalt almost seamless with vegetated shoulders and embankments. Large blocks of granite coping stones ("Rockefeller's teeth") served as rustic guardrails. Not too curvy, not too straight, the road brought the island's diverse features in sight.

Immediately the majority of visitors experienced Acadia from the Park Loop Road, while the wealthy took to the sea and air. Private yachts owned by some of the richest people in America stopped at Acadia. Their

The new parking area atop Cadillac Mountain, ca. 1934. ACADIA NATIONAL PARK

ACADIA NATIONAL PARK

MOTORISTS GUIDE

PARK LOOP ROAD

Twentieth-century guidebooks, like this one from 1989, focused on automobile travel. ACADIA NATIONAL PARK

sizes and power had grown, from Eliot's forty-three-and-a-half-foot sail-boat to megayachts hundreds of feet long.

Plane travel to Acadia began in 1934 with construction of the Bar Harbor Municipal Airport in Trenton. The Bar Harbor Chamber of Commerce promoted the airport as a way for visitors to increase their time on the island while also staying close to business at home. Private jets swooped into Acadia alongside the growing lines of traffic along the mainland Route 3.

More and more visitors driving on the Park Loop Road accelerated deterioration of the roadway and adjacent park areas, which in turn affected the experience of visitors. On a busy August day, more than 5,000 people in 1,500 vehicles—cars, RVs, motor coaches, tour buses— could create traffic jams on the Cadillac Mountain Road. The roads were not designed for the turning radii and space needs of large motor-coach buses. Exhaust combined with worsening regional air quality created hazy conditions on the summit.

Something had to be done to address the traffic and air pollution. In 1999 Friends of Acadia, working with the National Park Service and others, with three million dollars in grants from Maine outdoors outfitter L.L.Bean, launched a fleet of eight propane-fueled buses, the first national park shuttle system outside of Alaska. Hundreds of people seized the chance for a free ride on one of the seven routes around Mount Desert Island, immediately filling the "Island Explorer" buses to capacity. The service expanded the following year.

Water was still the only route to Isle au Haut. Thirty-foot lobster boats had been carrying mail, freight, and paid passenger traffic from Stonington to the town dock at the Thoroughfare, with occasional stops at Duck Harbor. Both full-time and seasonal residents were content with the boat service, as any increase would inevitably bring more tourists and associated development.

As the twentieth century came to a close, people began arriving at Mount Desert Island again via water. At Bar Harbor, visitors stepped onto the town dock from cruise ships, part of itineraries that included Halifax, St. John, Quebec City, Portland, Boston, and Newport.

At first, in the 1980s, about twenty ships came each summer; by 1993 the number had grown to forty-five vessels, including the *Queen Elizabeth II*, the largest cruise ship in the world. Following global trends, more and more people arrived this way each year, from twenty-five thousand cruise ship passengers in the 1990s to more than one hundred thousand (aboard more than a hundred ships) in the 2000s.

The ships anchored offshore and ferried passengers ashore in smaller "tender" boats. After a fifteen-minute ride to the Bar Harbor pier, many then boarded an air-conditioned motor-coach bus for touring the park.

The vessels and vehicles of arrival may have changed, but the experience of reaching destination Acadia did not. Bar Harbor and Southwest Harbor, Winter Harbor and the Thoroughfare, remained the primary points of entry from the water. Everyone else, including those landing at the airport in Trenton or Bangor, arrived on Mount Desert Island by road, from the north via Route 3.

Sometime after the sprawling city of Ellsworth, after aging strip malls and T-shirt outlets, ice-cream stands, family restaurants, and miniature golf, somewhere near the airport, visitors got their first glimpse of the park: the *Isle des Monts Déserts*, great rounded hills, their bare summits streaked with trees, granite shining in the sun.

Visitors were struck by how big the island looked, especially compared to the map that showed a cute and compact arrangement of towns, mountains, lakes, and harbors. *How immense an island it really is!* they thought. The same held true of Schoodic—so far out there, especially by road, east and down—and Isle au Haut, such a small island on the map, just a drop off the coast of Stonington, and yet the outermost island of the Penobscot Bay archipelago.

And then, finally at Trenton, the bridge over the narrows to the island and the ocean, aquamarine, with the spruce trees clinging to the rocks and the seagulls and the great blue herons in the marshes.

Arrived.

Navigation

How People Found Their Way Around Acadia

The man who lives in the interior of the country has very little to remind him of the Federal Government under which he lives. But go with me upon the crest of any one of these hills and look seaward; upon every headland a light-house; upon every sunken ledge, a buoy or spindle. The safe channel along the whole coast is clearly marked; and when the fog curtain falls, the Nation does not forget its children upon the water, but guides them to safety by signals.

—Honorable L. B. Deasy, at the dedication of
Sieur de Monts National Monument

When fog falls on Cadillac Mountain, gray fills the space between here and there, erasing the background. There is only foreground. Vision useless, all other senses awaken: the smell of sweet fern and balsam fir; the faint warning sound of the buoy bell at the ledge; the taste of salt in the air; the cool drip of condensed fog on the skin. Fog is as characteristic of Acadia as granite and spruce. It rolls in off the ocean, surrounds the islands, fills the harbors, and wraps the peaks in disorienting blankness.

No one feared the fog more than mariners, who approached Acadia's ledge-strewn shores with both trepidation and delight. They knew the hills of Mount Desert as a prominent landmark. They could sight Cadillac Mountain from sixty miles away. The sunlight reflecting off the hills were welcome signs; fishermen knew Sargent Mountain as Brassy Mountain because of its color as seen from the sea.

In the era before maps or charts, sailors steered by other fixtures: stars, currents, the scent of land. With each angle, Acadia presented a different view, each summit revealed and hidden in turn. It was a sight for the sore eyes of John Winthrop's crew in 1630. They'd been at sea for two months; a pregnant passenger had just had a miscarriage the day before. They yearned for land.

About three in the afternoon, we had sight of land to the northwest about ten leagues, which we supposed was Monhegan but it proved Mansell [Mount Desert]. Then we tacked and stood west southwest. We had now fair sunshine weather, and so pleasant a sweet air as did much refresh us, and there came a smell off the shore like the smell of a garden.

European explorers featured Acadia on early maps of the "new world." Samuel de Champlain was the first to delineate the coast from Nova Scotia to Cape Cod. On assignment from trading company leader Sieur de Monts to find sites for French settlement south of St. Croix Island, he sailed west in a forty-foot *patache* with a crew of twelve plus two Native American guides in September 1604.

Champlain advanced through thick fog, sounding the depths with lead line, skirting the islands and rounding Schoodic Point. He wrote in his journal:

That same day we also passed near an island about four or five leagues in length . . . It is very high and cleft in places, giving it the appearance from the sea of seven or eight mountains one alongside the other. The tops of most of them are bare of trees, because there is nothing there but rocks. The woods consist only of pines, firs, and birches. I named it l'isle des Monts-déserts.

He sailed north and documented that Mount Desert was indeed an island, not a peninsula as it had been previously portrayed. He sailed back along the shore, the mountains casting long shadows in the late afternoon light. The ship scraped ledge and began to take on water. Seeking refuge, Champlain steered into Otter Cove to inspect and repair the damage.

He continued his island survey over the next few days and noted smoke from Wabanaki fires. The Native people came out and traded fish and beaver for French biscuit and "sundry other trifles" and told Champlain they could take him to see their chief up the Penobscot. As he followed them, Champlain named "another high and striking island" *Isle au Haut*. Mount Desert and Isle au Haut would be the only names given by Champlain in the region to survive.

Based on this voyage and others in the two following years, Champlain drew a portolan chart of the Acadia region on vellum, with compass directions and shoreline features, embellished with a decorative wind rose and divided into thirty-two rhumb lines. He outlined the Gulf of Maine, emphasizing the major rivers, bays, and islands and Wabanaki villages along the shore and head of tide. Tiny dots denoted shoals, anchors more dangerous areas requiring stopovers. Unlike many "explorers" working under the doctrine of discovery, who benefited from portraying the New World as empty of people, Champlain was honest in his dealings with and representations of the Native people. Nor did he speculate on what he saw.

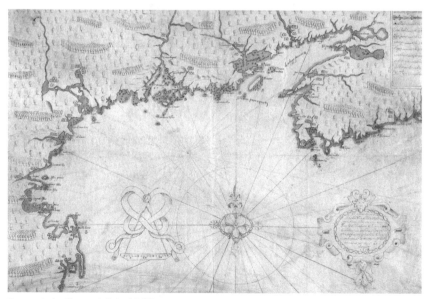

Samuel de Champlain's 1607 map. LIBRARY OF CONGRESS

Most charts of the time were drawn by professional cartographers who depended on information obtained from explorers, navigators, and cosmographers. In contrast, with much time and effort, Champlain boldly drew his chart based on his own exploration and observations. He used a compass and an astrolabe to determine distance and latitude, interviewed Native Americans, and applied scientific principles. Champlain's portrayal of Acadia was truthful and modern.

In the ensuing centuries of conflict among the Wabanaki Confederacy, Britain, France, and colonists, war and trade demanded nautical charts sketched by military engineers. Mount Desert's visibility from sea made it a rendezvous point for naval operations. Mapmakers assembled the collective experience and records of many navigators into descriptive guides and sailing charts.

British surveyor general Samuel Holland's land inspections included coastal regions, since that's where settlements were concentrated. His coastal surveys found their way into the hands of Joseph Frederick Wallet Des Barres, who surveyed the Atlantic coast and waters of North America for the British navy. Des Barres and his staff compiled new and previous information into the *Atlantic Neptune*, volumes of charts that were printed and bound on demand, resulting in multiple, variable editions. The full use of color gave the views an artistic excellence.

The first large-scale map of Mount Desert Island appeared as one of 180 maps in the *Atlantic Neptune* in 1781. Des Barres outlined the island, with Xs marking danger spots. Two additional charts roughly shaded the hills and showed depths of a few harbors and thoroughfares. They were charts designed for mariners, from the perspective of a ship at sea: rocks, ledges, and shoals, safe places to anchor.

Expanding settlements required detailed property maps. John Peters showed more detail of Mount Desert in his 1794 map, including mills and lakes, but mariners still relied on privately printed charts, most based on British work. The first truly American navigation atlases came from Edmund Blunt of Newburyport, Massachusetts. A successful journalist, Blunt was shocked by the inaccuracies in most of the existing navigation

From *Charts of the Coast and Harbors of New England,* 1776.
J. F. W. DES BARRES / BOSTON PUBLIC LIBRARY

guides, and retired from the newspaper business to publish the *American Coast Pilot,* which contained only text at first and still included remnants of the British guides. Blunt then published the *American Practical Navigator.* The "seaman's bible," the *Navigator* originated in Portugal in the sixteenth century and was translated into English by, among others, Richard Eden, for whom the town of Eden was named (and later renamed Bar Harbor).

Blunt was eager to improve upon the best-selling British version and felt a responsibility to the young nation. He asked Nathaniel Bowditch, a well-known mathematician and skilled navigator, to revise the manual and correct the numerous errors throughout. First published in 1802, Bowditch's *New American Practical Navigator* could be read and understood by most sailors. It would be published continuously for the next 150 years. Bowditch's fame would compel Isle au Haut residents to extend a welcome mat to his descendant, landscape architect Ernest Bowditch, when he founded the Point Lookout summer colony in 1881.

The *American Coast Pilot* evolved from the many books of sailing directions compiled over the centuries, revised and amended over time. Containing courses and distances from Boston to the Mississippi River, the *Coast Pilot* printed by Blunt in 1804 was the first edition with engraved charts and data from harbor surveys that Blunt himself paid for.

For example, to get from Long Island (Frenchboro) to Mount Desert:

> *If you are in a large vessel and make the Isle au Haut; bring the said island to bear W. S. W. and steer E. N. E. 10 leagues, which course and distance will carry you up the eastern passage going into Mount-Desert: You must leave all the islands to the northward, and go to the northward of Mount-Desert-Rock . . . In going from Mount-Desert to Goldsboro, you must steer N. N. E. for Skutock-Hills, which lie to the N. N. E. of that part, which are remarkable from any hills in the Eastern country . . . There are five of these hills, and at a distance they appear round.*

In 1837 Captain Seward Porter's nine charts of the Coast of Maine detailed islands and shoreline features. Produced by Thomas Moore's lithography shop in Boston, Porter charts indicated depths in Somes Sound and around the Cranberry Isles and showed the rocks and ledges of Isle au Haut. But blank space still dominated the ocean, and errors persisted in existing maps and guides. Reported in the daily news, shipwrecks were common, and costly for insurance companies, prompting

President Thomas Jefferson to create the Survey of the Coast in 1807 to provide nautical charts for America's growing ports and busy coastline.

Before they could position survey vessels at sea to measure water depths and map underwater hazards like rocks and reefs, federal surveyors first had to establish known positions on land. They also wanted to create a consistent, standardized system of mapping and charting.

Beginning in New York, reconnaissance teams—including Blunt's son Edward—spread north and south along the East Coast to search for locations that could be used as common reference points. By 1850 they had worked their way north to Acadia, scoping out potential locations to serve as benchmarks at Isle au Haut and Mount Desert.

Surveyors used triangulation, baselines, and night sky observations to measure and map adjacent areas, applying basic trigonometry at a landscape scale. In triangulation, surveyors set permanent survey marks and measured the horizontal angles between the marks. If the angles between three points were known, and the distance between two of the points measured precisely (a baseline), then the distances to the other points could be calculated. Each side of the triangle became the side of a new one, a chain of triangles from Maine to Louisiana eventually forming the backbone of every map and chart produced by the US government.

After ascending the "heavily timbered" summit on Isle au Haut, Edward Goodfellow and Stephen Harris used the North Star and the Big Dipper to align their sight with other stations. These observations, often numbering in the hundreds, allowed surveyors to determine latitude and a location's position on the globe. As they moved north and east, the summit of Green (Cadillac) was an obvious place to reference in maps and charts.

Sometime around 1853 the Coast Survey contracted with Richard Hamor of Bar Harbor to build a cabin on the mountain to house the workers. The Coast Survey archives contain no record of the construction. According to historian Richard Hale in *The Story of Bar Harbor*:

In 1853, when it was planned to erect a survey station on the top of Green Mountain, Richard Hamor of Eden was commissioned to build "in a sheltered place near the top" a "house 10 x 12 square & 9 feet high of boards battened with 3 x 1 inch battens on the roof and

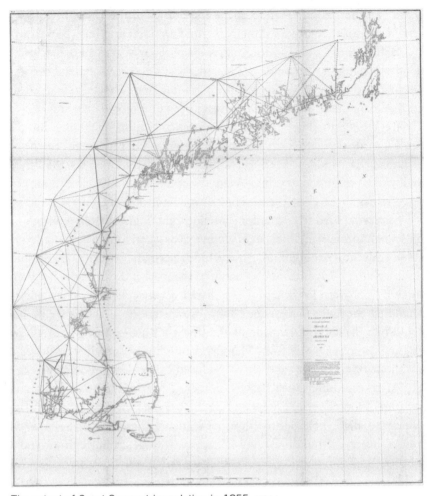

The extent of Coast Survey triangulation in 1855. NOAA

sides, floored with table & 2 bunks inside, to have one window with
8 lights and a sliding shutter or deadlight outside to secure it." For
this Deputy Collector of Customs Daniel E. Somes, of Mount Desert,
Maine, was instructed to pay Mr. Hamor $50. Likewise, Artificer
Thomas McDonnell, of the Coast Survey, hacked out a usable road, up
which a team could drag the survey instruments to the top of Green
[Cadillac] Mountain.

The Coast Survey structure atop Green [Cadillac] Mountain, ca. 1855. The structure later was turned into an inn. ACADIA NATIONAL PARK

Assistant Charles O. Boutelle, of a Maine family, on August 6, 1853, erected a heliotrope some fifty-six feet high. A signal mirror that reflected sunlight in a precise luminous point to observers twenty, forty, even one hundred miles away, the heliotrope worked in all but the foggiest, rainiest days. Boutelle flashed light to his coworkers, who stood with a heavy, high-precision telescope at Camden Hills or Dixmont. Boutelle then recorded the angles between the new station and the established ones.

Much of this work was carried out under the direction of Alexander Dallas Bache. Born in Philadelphia, the great-grandson of Benjamin Franklin, Bache first came to Acadia in July 1822, while a student at the US Military Academy at West Point.

The *New York Daily Advertiser* reported:

Captain Bache, of the corps of Topographical Engineers, embarked on Sunday last, in the sloop Packet, for Maine, pursuant to the orders from the Military Department. The object of this expedition is to visit Mount Desert and the adjacent country, to ascertain what advantages it offers for the erection of forts and other military establishments. It is unnecessary to enlarge upon the utility of this enterprise. We would only remark, that the appointment of a gentleman of so much skill and talents affords every assurance that the object of government will be completely effected. He is assisted by Lieutenant Eakins, Graham, and Boice, of the Artillery.

Bache served three years in the Army Corps of Engineers and then taught natural history and chemistry at the University of Pennsylvania. Ever ambitious, he was appointed superintendent of the Coast Survey in December 1843. During his term with the Coast Survey, Bache helped form the National Academy of Sciences and served as its first president.

Bache came back to Maine in the 1850s when the Coast Survey established triangulation points east of the Kennebec. He journeyed Downeast to see what mountains would be most helpful and, of course, found himself on "Mount Desert"—Green (Cadillac) Mountain.

In August 1856 he and Edward Goodfellow joined a crew that had been working at Saunders Mountain in Dedham. They marked the top of Green (Cadillac) Mountain with a copper bolt.

Coast Survey party working near Mount Desert, 1862. C. ROCKWELL/NOAA

Bache made many of the angle observations himself: east to Isle au Haut, Ragged Mountain, and Dixmont; north to Dedham; east to Humpback (Lead) Mountain; a dozen lines of sight leading to dozens more to dozens more. Bache's observations for the first time allowed for the determination of the geographical position of Mount Katahdin. Stephen Harris and Goodfellow, moving slightly northeast to a spot marked by a heavy granite block, used a zenith telescope to observe the position of the stars and determine latitude.

Almost immediately after the Coast Survey built the trail to the summit, hikers began using it, and the surveyor's building and its inhabitants became a curiosity worthy of mention in traveler's accounts.

Charles Tracy, in the diary of his 1855 visit, remembered his party of seventeen-plus-guide setting out "with basket, pail, shawl & sunshade" to walk up the mountain by the surveyors road. "First it took us through a broad woods, then up a hillside with green grass and scattered trees, then up the stoney side of the bare mountain." They paused often to rest, "seated about on stones and mosses."

He continued, "The very top of this rock pile is surmounted by the observatory of the coast survey, and a surveyor was there, in his thick box coat, taking directions of endless series of land marks visible from this commanding point. We stopped at his shanty, where he passes the storms and the nights."

The station was occupied until 1860, when the commercial Green Mountain House was built and the path improved into a road. Coast Survey crews continued to use the station for secondary triangulation through 1865.

Only after elevation benchmarks and triangulation stations were established did the Coast Survey begin hydrographic surveys, mapping the shoreline and charting the bottom of rivers and harbors. Over the next twenty-five years, the region surrounding Mount Desert Island was surveyed in detail.

Hydrographic crews sounded the depths of Massachusetts Bay and Boston Harbor as the triangulators pushed Downeast. By 1859 the oblique arc continuous from Acadia to Cape Fear, the underwater mapping extended to Mount Desert Rock.

North Summit and Face of Echo Mt.Mt.Desert.Id.(From South Summit.)

Coast Survey cartographer Edwin Hergesheimer accompanied the survey crews, informing the accuracy of their work with illustrations, as in this 1883 drawing of Echo [Beech] Mountain. NOAA

At the same time, they reported potential locations for lighthouses to the Lighthouse Board. Assistant T. A. Craven reported on Isle au Haut:

This harbor is much resorted to by the fishing fleets as a harbor of refuge. It is open to the southwest, and the light on Saddle Back ledge, about six miles distant, shows fair into the harbor; and I think no other is needed, but would recommend, instead of a light-house at the thoroughfare, that one be placed on the dry ledge lying northeast by north from the easternmost of the Spoon islands, distant about half a mile, where it would be a guide to coasters bound up Jericho bay . . . It would connect with the light on Mount Desert Rock, and warn vessels of the proximity of several dangerous ledges—especially the fatal "Black Ledges," which lie nearly four miles east by south from the northern part of Isle au Haut, and which have proved very sadly disastrous to vessels caught here in bad weather.

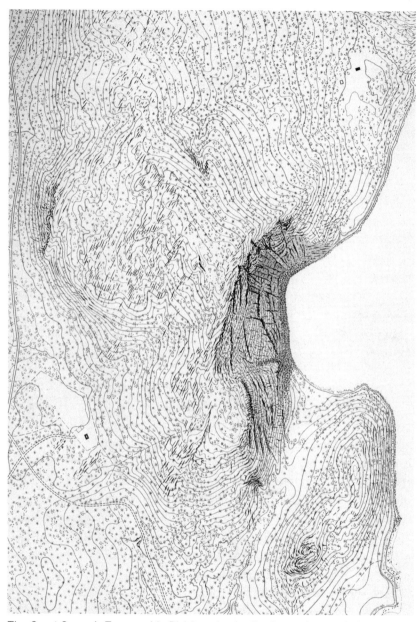

The Coast Survey's Topographic Division standardized mapping symbols and demonstrated how to interpret contours. Drawing of Eagle Cliff (St. Sauveur Mountain). E. HERGESHEIMER / NOAA

The US government constructed lighthouses on Baker Island in 1828, Bass Harbor in 1858, Egg Rock in 1875, and Robinson Point at Isle au Haut in 1907.

Beneficiaries of mapping, the early ferries to Acadia had a challenging time in this environment, relying on compass headings and local knowledge for direction, as described by David Granston in an article about steamboat travel to Mount Desert Island:

On her run between Rockland and Mount Desert, the J T Morse *had sixty-three compass heading changes, of which forty-five were only followed for a few seconds. Because of these constant course changes, it was important for captains to maintain well-calibrated compasses and to keep interfering metal objects at a distance in order to reduce the chances of missing a buoy. When metal did interfere with the compass it was often due to an unknowing lady leaning against the pilothouse [the metal in her corset stays tugging at the needle]. In foggy weather, the captain relied on the echo of the steamer's whistle as well as the sound of nearby bell buoys and lighthouse foghorns to help guide him along the way.*

In 1867 the Coast Survey published the first large-scale chart of the Acadia region, showing harbor depths, islands and lighthouses, and land features along the Schoodic Peninsula. Work continued into the 1870s. Survey crews were engaged in triangulation, topography, and charting in Bass Harbor, Blue Hill Bay, and east Penobscot Bay, including Isle au Haut and the eastern side of Mount Desert. Assistant J. W. Donn surveyed the waters around Mount Desert with the schooner *Scoresby*. In one season they covered 69 miles of shoreline, 41 square miles of topography, nearly 4,000 angles, and 18,293 soundings. Each sounding, made by lowering a weighted hemp rope or wire over the side of the ship, was tied to the copper bolt benchmark on Cadillac.

The survey released a topographic map for Mount Desert Island in its entirety in 1875. The map looks different from those that came before: The island is tilted eastward, enhancing the alignment of the mountain summits and intervening valleys. To help guide the printing process,

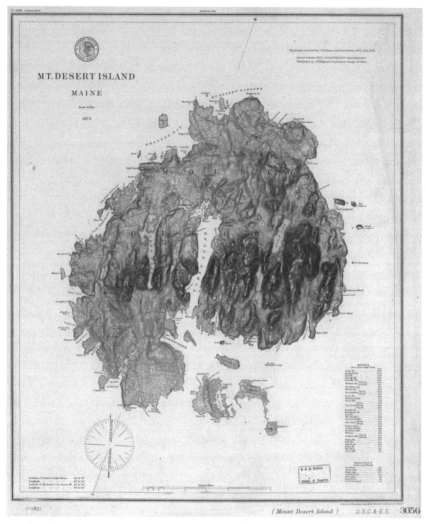

The first complete map of Mount Desert Island, 1875. E. HERGESHEIMER / NOAA

assistant Edwin Hergesheimer drew common features of the East Coast, using Robinson (Acadia) and Brown (Norumbega) Mountains, Eagle Cliff, and Echo Mountain to illustrate eroded and fractured granite. Topographic and hydrographic data were combined in an 1883 navigation chart for Mount Desert Island, Blue Hill Bay, and Frenchman Bay.

Coast Survey maps and data became the foundation for other maps in the nineteenth and early twentieth centuries, which became more oriented toward tourists and the growing summer community on Mount Desert Island and focused more on speculation than navigation. Unlike navigational maps and charts, early property maps outlined parcel shape and size, and who "owned" which land.

County maps and atlases showed landownership as well as businesses and services. One of the earliest, H. F. Walling's 1860 Topographical Map of Hancock County for the first time showed roads, residences, and commercial establishments and delineated town boundaries with insets of villages. As this was a map for getting around town and finding schools, churches, fish houses, and other businesses, the ocean was left blank—nothing there to buy or visit. The 1887 Colby & Stuart Map combines roads and residences with property parcels, mountain topography, ferry routes, hotels, and scenic features.

Historian George Street noted that "many maps are issued by the transportation companies and the land companies, and are contained in the guidebooks, but most of them are very inaccurate." According to the Coast Survey, this confusion resulted from the East Coast's complicated history.

Compared to the Gulf and Pacific coasts, in the East the Wabanaki, Norse, Spanish, English, French, Dutch, Swedish, etc., built their own interacting systems of geography and naming. In the Coast Survey's 1856 annual report, mapper J. G. Kohl reported to Superintendent Bache, "As settlements followed or displaced each other, the names of places have accumulated. Old designations have been, in some cases, obliterated by new ones, and the records of their history have either been lost or scattered through the great mass of provincial and local documents yet extant in the archives of historical societies in different towns and state capitals along the coast."

The constantly changing place names frustrated Edward Rand, who felt existing maps did not correlate with his own intimate knowledge of Acadia's landscape and place names. So, as part of *Flora of Mount Desert*

Island, he created a new map using Coast Survey data and place names "based on the most trustworthy authorities." He removed the property ownership and settlements, but kept the roads. A topographical map of island elevations, labeled with land and ocean place names, also showed the footpaths in the vicinity of Northeast Harbor and Jordan Pond. Accuracy mattered to Rand and his audience, who believed it necessary to know the names of lakes and hills, the stories behind the names, and the routes to get there.

In the decades before the park was established, the village improvement societies—civic organizations concerned with infrastructure and beautification—took on the responsibilities of building, maintaining, and mapping trails. To help hikers find their way, they replaced rock piles and upright stone trail markers with more complex cairns. Edward Rand continued to work with trail builders Waldron Bates and Herbert Jaques to update what became known as the "Path Map." The 1901 version was the first to identify trail names; revised versions accompanied a comprehensive guide for the island's walking paths.

Maps changed again after the formation of the Hancock County Trustees of Public Reservations and the first parcels of land were conserved. William Sherman's 1911 map depicted roads, footpaths, town lines, and the boundaries of "public reservations" around the Bowl and Beehive, Green (Cadillac) Mountain, and the Jordan Pond area. Each successive update had more green shading, a reflection of the expanding protected area that became the national park.

Then things got confusing again when George Dorr, then the first superintendent of Acadia, decided to change the names of the Mount Desert hills. To Dorr, the existing "descriptive" names assigned by early settlers and summer visitors—Brown, Dry, Green—were not old or distinctive enough. Dorr wanted place names to conjure the island's French history as well as recognize the Native people, the Wabanaki. The new names would serve as historic documents, recording the human background of the park to succeeding generations. Without soliciting public input, and disregarding local protest, Dorr officially changed the names beginning in 1918.

Green Mountain became Cadillac Mountain. Newport Mountain became Champlain Mountain. Pickett became Huguenot Head. Dry

Edward L. Rand's 1893 map of Mount Desert Island, the first to combine topography, roads, and trails. LIBRARY OF CONGRESS

became Flying Squadron (later renamed Dorr); Little Brown's, Parkman; Robinson, Acadia; Dog, St. Sauveur; West Peak, Bernard; East Peak, Mansell. New mountain names meant trail names and their associated directional signs had to change, too. The new names appeared on the first US Geological Survey (USGS) map of the national park, published in 1922.

But the US government maps did not show any trails, prompting Harold Peabody to reference the old Rand maps as the best source for navigating Mount Desert Island trails in his 1928 hiking guide. Peabody also used the "old names," resisting the changes implemented by Dorr. Such local resistance led to a mix of old and new names on maps and signs, perpetuated when the Civilian Conservation Corps installed 780 new signs throughout the park. When the joint path committee published the first path map in 1896, they mounted and lacquered it onto boards for posting at major trail intersections. The need for orientation outlasted the map boards.

In 1938 Charles Savage spent $544 to build a small pavilion on his property, where the Asticou and Eliot Mountain trails intersected with Asticou Way. He hung a map on the wall, for use by all walkers and passersby who might need to orient themselves. The Map House was a favorite resting spot for the writer Willa Cather, who spent a number of summers at Asticou in the 1940s.

With the establishment of the park came "official" maps and guides. Towns and chambers of commerce simultaneously published map brochures to aid visitors. The park's 1935 guidebook had a map showing the roads on the eastern side of Mount Desert; the first separate map appeared in 1949, without hiking trails but showing parking boundaries and roads. The path committees had a lessened role, with the last path maps printed in 1941. The USGS finally added the trail system, with slight variations in names and locations, to its topographical map in 1942.

Park management changed "guidance" signage, replacing markers with new ones, removing or not maintaining cairns. In the late 1950s, Mission 66 crews replaced the CCC trail signs, with many original names changed or spelled wrong. Locals continued to use the "old names," travel abandoned trails, and, like the "phantom signmaker" in Bar Harbor, post their own directional signs, ensuring confusion for tourists for decades.

The complexity of the waters around Acadia continued to confound navigators in the twentieth century, especially when locked in one of the region's frequent fogs. In August 1992 the cruise ship *Queen Elizabeth II* anchored off Bar Harbor, the fog preventing passengers and crew from getting to shore. A navigational chart could not be too detailed. To assist the increasing number of cruise ships, which shared the waters with private yachts, whale-watching boats, and commercial fishermen, Bar Harbor worked with the Coast Guard to update charts, establishing traffic lanes and marking major fishing grounds in an effort to keep the two enterprises separate.

As late as 2002 the park was still working with publishers to ensure the accuracy of maps and trail guides, although available options were good enough to allow the park to cease producing its own trail map.

——

With more than thirty-five thousand acres, and another twelve thousand under conservation easement, Acadia National Park includes land on Mount Desert Island, Isle au Haut in Penobscot Bay, Schoodic Point, and a number of outlying islands. Acadia is much larger than it seems. On a map, the summits appear close together, their sides so steep the topographic lines blur deceptively into shading. From any one location, it is easy to underestimate time and distance. The ocean, too, is larger than it seems. Maps and charts confuse as much as they clarify.

Clear signals make it through the fog. The buoy bell clangs, the island tower flashes its light, and across the exposed summits of Cadillac and other mountains, stacked stones show the way home.

Study

Acadia's Scientific Roots

Hark, the sound of song comes faintly from the distance, and we hear
Louder growing every moment the resounding C.S. cheer.
Here comes the scientific offerings, here come tributes gained by toil,
Long reports of all knowledge gained upon Mt. Desert's soil!
—John McGau Foster, member of the
Champlain Society

It was the fifth of July, the year 1880. The forty-four-foot sloop *Sunshine* lay at anchor in Wasgatt Cove, where a small brook emptied into Somes Sound. On shore, in a field just north of Asa Smallidge's house, eight young men were cutting the grass and setting up canvas tents. From the boat they unloaded shotguns and nets, fishing rods and glass bottles, small wooden boxes and stacks of books and notepaper. They cut a sapling into a pole and raised a red, white, and blue flag while cheering, "Yo-ho! Yo-ho! Yo-ho!"

Under the leadership of "Captain" Charles Eliot, son of Harvard president Charles W. Eliot, the students were on the island for the summer, each having committed to do some work in some branch of natural history or science. They called the camp Pemetic, after a Wabanaki name for the place, and called themselves the Champlain Society, after the European explorer who renamed Mount Desert Island in 1604. They would be just as lofty in their goals and dedicated in their service to the landscape.

The next day, July 6, a southeasterly storm prevented work on the campsite or their individual scientific "specialties." Reflecting the evolution of science, with the broader field of "natural history" splitting into more narrow disciplines, the students divided themselves into departments: botany, ornithology, lepidoptery, ichthyology, marine biology, geology, and meteorology.

The rain ended in the afternoon. They fashioned tables of rough-cut lumber; on one, they erected a meteorological box, a cabinet containing instruments such as a thermometer and barometer. William H. Dunbar began to work on flowers. Henry Spelman went out to "sample" (shoot) birds, and photographer Marshall Slade prepared glass negative plates.

Charles and Samuel Eliot had been visiting the area since they were young, sailing and camping with their father. Their father and stepmother went to Europe in 1880, leaving the boys the yacht and camping gear to use with their friends.

Over the next two months, helped by locals and guided by DeCosta's *Rambles on Mount Desert*, Dodge's *Mount Desert and the Cranberry Isles*, and Drake's *Nooks and Corners of the New England Coast*, the young men made daily excursions, on foot and by boat, around Mount Desert Island. They collected plants and birds; dredged starfish, sea cucumbers, and other small animals from the bottom of Somes Sound; caught mackerel and flounder for food. They stared at the rocks along shore, took photographs, wrote poems and letters.

They could be found roaming the woods morning, noon, and night, walking along the dirt roads, bushwhacking to Jordan Pond, hiking the nearby mountains. Every few days they sailed to Southwest Harbor for the mail and provisions, or to pick up or drop off a club member at the ferry landing. They sailed to the Cranberries and other islands.

At night they played cards (cribbage and whist, a trick-taking game similar to spades), analyzed the day's samples, read novels, and wrote letters. They documented their activities in daily logbooks, kept running lists of species collected, and developed a map of the island, adding trails and woods roads as they encountered them.

Back at Harvard during the school year, they shared reports and memories from the past summer's work and planned future seasons. They presented their findings before both the Boston and Harvard natural history societies. And they detailed their activities and scientific findings in a series of journals, preserved in the collection of the Mount Desert Island Historical Society.

If the Champlain Society had been somewhat quiet in 1880 (as suggested by their journals), they made their presence known in 1881. On the evening of July Fourth, after setting up camp, "the committee on pyrotechnics gave a display to a large and enthusiastic audience from North East Harbor, in fact the whole village apparently." Fireworks, songs, torchlight processions, and calls of "Yo-ho!" echoed across Somes Sound throughout the summer.

In 1882 the Champlain Society decided not to hire a cook, due to the expense, and so was forced to move its camp closer to amenities. Camp Asticou was established at the head of Northeast Harbor near the inn of A. C. Savage, where members ate meals for five dollars per week. This location was closer to the Eliot family's new summer home—the "Ancestral Mansion"—on the eastern shore of the harbor, where young Charles and Sam could usually be found when not visiting camp or

The Champlain Society poses for a photograph at Hadlock Brook, 1881. M. P. SLADE/ MOUNT DESERT ISLAND HISTORICAL SOCIETY

joining Champlain Society members on walks and sails. The relocation made the society more visible. They regretted the arrival of boarders at Savage's and the subsequent loss of privacy that left them "not alone in their glory as they would wish."

The society continued their surveys of island flora and fauna, although to a lesser degree, as socializing began to preempt science.

Sunday July 23rd . . . A little incident deserves mention in this log: While Spelman was alone in camp this afternoon a buckboard passed by on the road. Said a lady to the driver, "Why, what is this camp here?" "It is the Harvard camp; the camp where the Harvard boys are staying," replied the driver. "Harvard boys! rather Harvard barbarians!" said the lady. It has come to this at last,—if we do not live at Bar Harbor, or at least in a hotel we are called barbarians! Probably the lady was thinking of the derivation of the word, and applied it to Townsend, for his beard is becoming more like a forest, and less like stunted scrub growth every day. . . .

Sunday July 30th . . . This afternoon the conduct of many of the buckboarders was most unseemly. The campers were fairly driven into the parlor tent by the frantic demonstrations of one buckboard, and soothed by the sweet singing of another party that stopped in front of the camp while singing, and then informed us that the music was not intended for our benefit. Such conduct in strangers shocks the camp very much. . . .

They were unique for camping, as most visitors at the time stayed in hotels or boardinghouses. Recreational camping in Acadia emerged much later, in parallel with the arrival of the automobile.

While the destination of Mount Desert Island may have been unusual for a camping expedition, the Champlain Society otherwise followed a trend among college students. The pedestrian summer camping trip with a group of one's fellow students had become a well-established college pattern by midcentury. The Harvard "vacation ramble" was an extracurricular activity encouraged to make up for the lack of organized athletic programs and facilities.

Members of the Champlain Society at work on their "specialties," 1881. M. P. SLADE/
MOUNT DESERT ISLAND HISTORICAL SOCIETY

Members of the Champlain Society were not the first students to do summer fieldwork in Acadia. In 1860 Nathaniel Shaler and William Stimpson, students of Louis Agassiz at Harvard, made a summer dredging expedition along the eastern Maine coast. They used a small rowboat with a sail to get offshore, and then used the oars to pull a metal rake across the seafloor. As the drag came to the surface, Stimpson performed his ritual of a song:

> I was born upon the water and had ne'er a mother fairer,
> And for mother's milk my father gave me only old Madeira;
> So following out my early training I wander still upon the sea,
> But water yet I ne'er have tasted; water is no drink for me.
> Water, no, no, no; water, no, no, no,
> Water is no drink for me.

Marine biologist William Stimpson. SMITHSONIAN

He then took a swig of rum and cheered, "Here's to the haul!" The young biologists then picked out the treasures, inventorying species familiar and new.

Later that summer Shaler continued on to Mount Desert, where he met up with Addison Emery Verrill and Alpheus Hyatt. They did more dredging in Frenchman Bay, then from Trenton took a tent and camping gear to Bar Harbor. They hid the boat in the bushes by the waterfront and spent some days exploring Mount Desert Island. They camped at the base of Green (Cadillac) Mountain and hiked to the summit, a great event in Shaler's life, "for it brought my feet for the first time upon a mountain-top," he recalled in his autobiography.

Climbing the Mount Desert hills allowed Shaler to correspond observations in nature with his textbook knowledge. He recalled these personal experiences years later when taking his students on "field day" treks about greater Cambridge and when organizing summer field courses in geology. Shaler would return to the island in the 1870s and '80s in the service of the United States government.

The addition of science gave purpose and intensity to a summer afield. It wasn't enough to merely witness sublime and famous scenery. In the Victorian era, the traveler had to engage. As Rebecca Bedell wrote in *The Anatomy of Nature*, "With a botanical guide in his pocket and a rock hammer in his pack, the scientifically engaged traveler minutely inspected his environment, categorizing its manifold components and picking up specimens to press in his albums or mount in his mineral cabinet."

Thus Arlo Bates informed fellow travelers about Isle au Haut in *Outing* magazine:

> *Its flora is unusually rich and varied, its orchids being especially interesting; while it has butterflies enough to afford opportunity for the entomologist to render himself thoroughly obnoxious to all his friends for at least one season. Less scientifically inclined visitors have every chance to follow the universal sea-shore diversions of drying unfortunate starfishes and sea urchins, of gathering shells and sea-moss, and all that varied and useless assortment of curiosities which smell so ill, and which one is so utterly at a loss what to do with on going away. Sea-cucumbers come up on the fish-hooks now and then, and here and there one stumbles upon a stray whale's rib on the beach; and in short the island lacks none of the childlike joys of the seashore in general.*

With varying membership but with Charles Eliot always their "captain," the Champlain Society returned to Mount Desert each summer throughout the next decade, in the process compiling the first thorough natural history surveys of Acadia, including plants, birds, insects, fish, and marine invertebrates. Their geology professor, William Morris Davis, joined them at the camp in 1880 and 1881, but the students organized the expeditions and resulting scientific work themselves.

The Champlain Society followed in the footsteps of geologists, marine biologists, and the Coast Survey. Botanists, biologists, and archaeologists all studied the region in the second half of the nineteenth century, but except for the coast surveyors, who were not focused on natural history, all of these people spent at most only a few days or weeks in Acadia.

The Champlain Society, in contrast, spent at least eight weeks in Acadia every summer between 1880 and 1889, with Charles Eliot, Samuel Eliot, and Edward Rand spending even more time. They repeatedly and intensively focused on the biodiversity of a single place, and at the same time they were interested in the place in its entirety. They left a record that twenty-first century scientists would use to understand changes in the Acadia environment.

In 1888, the final summer of Champlain Society activities, Edward Rand and John C. Redfield, an attorney and summer resident who had built his own botanical collection, began working together to compile and consolidate botanical discoveries. In 1894 they published *Flora of Mount Desert Island, Maine*, documenting nearly 1,500 plant species, which included a report of the Champlain Society Geological Department by Professor William Morris Davis.

Henry Spelman maintained the bird list compiled by him and the other members of the Champlain Society Ornithological Department (Charles W. Townsend, Robert B. Worthington, and Julius Wakefield), which eventually made it into the hands of ornithologist Francis H. Allen.

In their journals, the students lamented the spread of tourism and its effect on the island. As early as 1881, in the first annual report of the Botanical Department, Edward Rand wrote:

Mt. Desert is, in beauty and diversity of scenery, the most attractive spot on the Eastern Coast of the United States. Nowhere else can be found such a combination of strait and streamlet, bay and lake, seashore and mountain as exist in this island. Therefore it naturally has become a famous and fashionable summer resort for people from all parts of the country. While this increasing popularity of the Island means prosperity to the inhabitants, it means destruction to many of

Nature's chiefest charms. Already the woods are falling beneath the axe to give place to flimsy, barn-like hotels, the rarer wildflowers are disappearing, the ferns and mosses are torn from the spots they have so long adorned, the wood-roads are becoming dusty highways . . . the shy birds of the wood are every year being driven farther and farther into the recesses of the Island; the lakes and streams are being depopulated by the unscrupulous fisherman; the animals are either being driven away or destroyed. In such a state of things it will not be many years before all the wildness of Mt. Desert is gone forever, and in its stead we have the tinsel-glitter of a Long Branch, Coney Island, or Newport, depending on its air, its society, and its scenery to attract visitors, though even the scenery will suffer great harm in the future if the woods are destroyed, and unsightly buildings erected on beautiful sites. Perhaps I have drawn an exaggerated picture of the future of Mt. Desert, but it is often better to exaggerate than belittle the magnitude of a coming evil.

This concern inspired the Champlain Society to advocate for conservation of Mount Desert Island. Later in the same report, Rand writes:

Is it possible to protect the natural beauty of the island in any way? . . . A company of interested parties could buy at a small cost the parts of the Island less desirable for building purposes. To these they could add from time to time such of the more desirable lots as they could obtain control of either by purchase or by arrangement with the proprietor. This tract of land should then be placed in the charge of a forester and his assistants; the lakes and streams should be stocked with valuable fish; the increase of animals and birds encouraged; the growth of trees, shrubs, plants, ferns and mosses cared for. This park should be free to all. . . . I hope, however that we may have the pleasure before long of listening to a paper on this subject by one of its earnest advocates, "Captain" Charles Eliot.

After graduation from Harvard, Eliot had decided to join the new field of landscape architecture. His uncle, Robert Peabody, introduced him to Frederick Law Olmsted, who invited him to become an apprentice. Eliot continued to be involved with the Champlain Society as "Captain Emeritus."

In March 1884 the Champlain Society gathered at Harvard president Charles W. Eliot's house in Cambridge to discuss society activities for the upcoming summer. They concluded, "The scenery of Mount Desert is so beautiful and remarkable that no pains should be spared to save it from injury—to the end that many generations may receive all possible benefit and enjoyment from the sight of it." They formed a committee, at the suggestion of Charles Eliot, "to consider the question of the preservation of the scenery of Mt. Desert."

Eliot and Rand continued to advocate for conservation and, after Charles Eliot's untimely death in 1897, his father, Charles W. Eliot, with George Dorr, formed the Hancock County Trustees of Public Reservations (modeled after an organization Charles Eliot created in Massachusetts), which acquired the first landholdings that became Acadia National Park, some thirty-six years after the Champlain Society's first summer.

Thus the Champlain Society can be linked directly to the idea of conserving the ground they studied. While the spirit of American conservation may have originated a century before, few scientists were actively working to protect the places where they worked, giving science a unique role in the creation of Acadia National Park, and Acadia a prominent place in the history of land conservation.

George Dorr recognized the importance of Acadia to science, and vice versa. At the dedication ceremony for Sieur de Monts National Monument in 1916, Dorr said that the park should be "a sanctuary and protecting home" for the whole region's plant and animal life. "Make it this, and naturalists will seek it from the whole world over, and from it other men will learn similarly to cherish wild life in other places."

Dorr had support from scientists. Merritt Fernald, who was from Maine and chaired the Botany Department at Harvard, wrote in a letter in support of federal protection that Acadia was the best single area he knew for preserving and exhibiting a wide range of northeastern US plants.

Mount Desert offered similar opportunities for birdlife, according to Ernest Howe Forbush, state ornithologist of Massachusetts, who conducted a study of Acadia's birds. T. Gilbert Pearson, cofounder and secretary of the National Association of Audubon Societies, stated in his letter that in all the years his association had been engaged in seeking to establish refuges or sanctuaries for wild birdlife, "no area in the East of such importance to wild life, bird or other, has been set aside as sanctuary as that contained within the borders of the Sieur de Monts National Monument."

In their push to have the national monument expanded to national park status, Dorr, Forbush, and Fernald wrote in *National Geographic*:

> *The only way in which to conserve for the enjoyment and study of future generations any portions of our country which by good fortune are still somewhat in their natural condition is the reservation of all such tracts as may properly be set aside, with the explicit stipulation that they be left essentially in the hands of Nature herself to care for. This brings me to the crucial point: where is the best spot, if only a single spot can be thus preserved, for the perfection of this ideal? . . . As a single area within the possible reach of this hope, the Island of Mount Desert, with its adjacent islets and headlands, stands out as offering the greatest natural diversity.*

When President Woodrow Wilson established the national monument, he cited first the historic connection to Samuel de Champlain and then, in the same paragraph, "The topographic configuration, the geology, the fauna and the flora of the island, largely embraced within the limits of the Monument, also, are of great scientific interest."

For Dorr, speaking at the dedication of the national monument, the history of scientific work on the island foretold the park's future:

> *During the early summer, when I was at Washington working on this matter of the Park's establishment and was plunged for weeks*

together in its oppressive heat, it struck me what a splendid and useful thing it would be if we could provide down here, in a spot so full of biologic interest and unsolved biologic problems, so rich in various beauty and locked around by a cool northern sea, a summer camp—some simple summer home—for men of science working in the government bureaus, in the museums and universities. They would come down to work . . . on a fresh field of life, bird or plant or animal, and then go back invigorated, ready to do more valuable work the whole winter through in consequence of this climatic boon and stimulating change.

Ecologist Barrington Moore agreed:

Mount Desert Island exhibits features which are of unusual significance to the student of natural history . . . Scientists all over America are urging the preservation of natural areas for scientific study. In research on distribution, on the influence of environment upon plants and animals, and on adaptation, it is essential to have areas on which the flora and fauna can be found undisturbed by outside agencies. The creation of the Lafayette [Acadia] National Park on an island of such great interest as Mount Desert Island is, therefore, of the utmost importance to science.

Dorr encouraged other scientific endeavors on Mount Desert Island outside park boundaries, donating land to support the establishment of the Mount Desert Island Biological Laboratory at Salisbury Cove in 1921 and the Jackson Laboratory in 1929. And at Schoodic, John G. Moore's heirs had given his land to the Hancock County Trustees of Public Reservations in 1927 with the requirement that the land be kept "forever as a free public park or for other public purposes and for such other uses as are incidental to the same, including the promotion of biological and other scientific research."

Scientists from universities throughout the Northeast flocked to Mount Desert and the surrounding area. Many continued the collecting work of the nineteenth century, expanding lists of insects (Charles

W. Johnson of the Boston Society of Natural History); intertidal fauna (Duncan S. Johnson and Alexander F. Skutch of Johns Hopkins University); fireflies (Ulric Dahlgren of Mount Desert Island Biological Laboratory); wildflowers (Edgar Wherry); birds (Mrs. Franklin Anthony, Marion Pellew, Eleonora Morgan). William Procter conducted a survey of mollusks and later expanded to insects, recording more than 6,500 species.

As the field of ecology emerged as its own discipline, some scientists came to Acadia to understand the relationships between plants, animals, and their environment, studying intertidal food webs and plant zonation. In 1924 Clarence Cook (C. C.) Little, president of the University of Maine, held the first summer laboratory session in the Bar Harbor area with six students who studied natural history, building on work of Edgar Wherry and Barrington Moore relating soil conditions to plant and animal life.

This history of science in relationship to a national park is unique. Outside of Acadia, advances in ecological knowledge taking place by the late nineteenth century had little to do with the national park movement.

Not until 1929 did the National Park Service hold its first naturalist conference, when George M. Wright used his personal fortune to launch the Park Service's first professional wildlife research program. The naturalists noted that scientific data on the parks' natural history were almost infinitesimal. But the Park Service didn't see a need for scientific studies. "Had George Wright not offered to fund a survey," wrote park historian Richard Sellars, "the Service might well have waited many more years before initiating its own science programs."

Acadia's first naturalist, Arthur Stupka, initiated an ambitious naturalist program in 1932. A graduate of the Yosemite School of Field Natural History, Stupka employed the principles he learned in the intensive seven-week summer program of the importance of studying living organisms in their natural environment. Through campfire talks, illustrated lectures, guided hikes to the Cadillac summit, and deep-sea fishing excursions, Stupka shared Acadia's natural history with visitors. He also recorded observations of park weather, flora, and fauna in a series of publications titled *Nature Notes*. However, further scientific inquiry was beyond the capacity of Stupka and other park employees. Other national parks faced a similar situation.

In the 1940s, sixty years after the Champlain Society first began their natural history surveys of Mount Desert Island, the National Park Service recognized that they did not have adequate funding for in-house research and instead encouraged scientists and university students to use the parks as field laboratories. It took another few decades for this vision

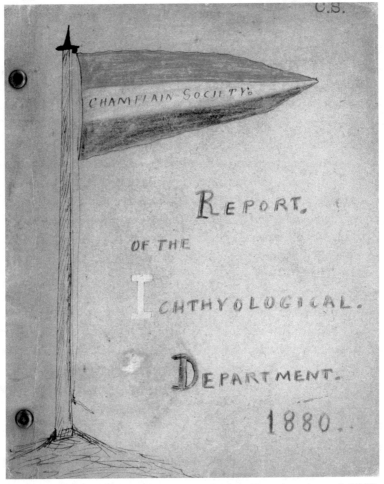

The cover of the Champlain Society's Ichthyology Department report, 1880.
MOUNT DESERT ISLAND HISTORICAL SOCIETY

to come to reality at Acadia, fostered by the founding of the College of the Atlantic. Under the leadership of professors William Drury and Craig Greene, College of the Atlantic students collected thousands of plants within the park, assisting with the first major study of the area's flora since 1929 and providing insight into changes in Mount Desert Island's plant life.

— ~

The stream of science carried on in Acadia, each research question building on the answers from an earlier time. So many currents can be traced back to the student members of the Champlain Society, who were in a place of stunning beauty and dramatic scenery at a crucial moment in their lives. They did not see themselves as tourists on a cursory visit. They were botanists, geologists, ichthyologists, meteorologists, entomologists, ornithologists, poets, artists, staying in one place for weeks or months at a time, every summer for nearly a decade. Imprinted with the sights, sounds, and smells of Acadia, they developed a "sense of place" that was key to their becoming catalysts for conservation.

More than a century later, a new generation is taking up the work of the Champlain Society, walking the same trails and comparing old data to new. They have a protected area in which to work, thanks in part to the Champlain Society's concern for the environment that led to the creation of a national park.

In the field where the Champlain Society first camped, owned by the Mount Desert Land & Garden Preserve, tall grasses and weeds conceal a narrow footpath to the water. Perhaps one day students will camp there again, forging bonds with each other—and a place called Acadia. Who knows what they might discover, what legacy they might leave?

Walking

Falling Under the Spell of Acadia's Trails

. . . as though we thought
that even our smallest gestures
would last forever.
—FROM THE POEM "DRAWING" BY CHRISTIAN BARTER

ONE HUNDRED FIFTY-THREE STEPS AND COUNTING, THE TRAIL ASCENDS a forest of birch and oak, meanders through jumbled boulders, under and around granite slabs, as if passing into another realm. The trail is narrow—two to three feet wide—and the rocks are close. Then, like magic, the trees give way to a sweeping view of a great meadow framed by giant white pines, fog rolling in from the ocean in the distance.

The trail continues.

Through another rock passageway, step number 300 is secured with iron pins. Made of the same stone that lines the trail and forms the mountainside, the steps clearly have been *placed*, and yet they, too, seem to blend like magic into their surroundings.

The fog, raked by spruces and hemlocks, condenses, drips from branch tips, and soaks the earth like rain that never fell. Bright kelly green algae and black lichen splotch the gray granite; ferns sprout from solid stone; the mist carries the scent of pine needles and huckleberries.

The tread of the path levels out, and at step 365, the Homans Path ends at an intersection, four hundred feet up the side of Dorr Mountain.

Crafted stone steps are characteristic of Acadia's trails.
ACADIA NATIONAL PARK

"Few natural areas of similar size offer as many trails with such a diversity of experiences as Acadia," declared a recent park-wide trail assessment. An understatement. A hiker at Acadia could be blown by gale-force winds atop a subalpine summit and an hour later be strolling along a quiet woodland path. One can walk from ocean surf to a beaver meadow, from downtown Bar Harbor to a pitch-pine-covered hill, from a lush stream valley to an exposed cliff.

Nothing in Acadia more exhibits the National Park Service mission to maintain spaces for "human use and enjoyment" than the trails—many, many miles of which exist within a relatively small park area. They bring the visitor into and through the landscape, enabling encounters with flora and fauna, water and earth. Yet to walk is also to participate in the human community of Acadia; no matter how wild a walk may seem, human history reveals itself: men and women with vision and might, horses and mallets, time and money, poetry and magic.

Throughout history, walking was the primary way people experienced Mount Desert Island. The experience went from a passive one created out of necessity to a highly contrived and constructed encounter. In 1901 the trail network was twice the size it is today, with some 250 miles of paths. Trail use declined after the 1947 fire and the rise of the automobile. The paths themselves deteriorated. By the time the renewed popularity of hiking sent more people onto Acadia's trails in an attempt to get "back to nature" in the 1970s, many trails were in rough shape.

When Gary Stellpflug started his job at Acadia in the summer of 1974, he faced collapsed retaining walls, washed-out trails, broken and disassembled steps, and confusing and missing signage. Beaver dams had flooded out sections of trail; decades of foot traffic had worn others to bare roots and mud.

The only full-time trail worker, with the help of one other seasonal staff, Stellpflug got to work addressing decades of neglect. Rather than reroute trails away from their original placement, he rebuilt them with log cribbing. He replaced bridges, cleaned blocked culverts, and invented a new, theft-proof style of directional sign using an engraved cedar post.

Lack of funds and staff continued to limit his progress, however. The trails finally got some attention in 1999, when the park and Friends of Acadia launched the Acadia Trails Forever campaign and raised thirteen million dollars to fund immediate and future work on the trail system.

Stellpflug faced a dilemma. With more than one hundred miles of lost or abandoned trails on Mount Desert Island, where should they start?

⁓

The Wabanaki created the first foot trails in Acadia as they portaged their canoes between lakes and wetlands to avoid rough coastal waters or reach inland resources. It is easy to see the logical places to traverse when looking at a map: from Pretty Marsh to Somes Sound via Round, upper Long, Ripple, and Somes Ponds. Eagle and Jordan Lakes connect to Hulls Cove and Seal Harbor; a similar route goes from Otter Creek to the Tarn and Cromwell Harbor Brook. The dangerous, exposed point at Schoodic can be avoided by portaging across the neck. Passages exist between Wonsqueak and Birch Harbors, and between West Gouldsboro, Jones Pond, and Gouldsboro.

The Native people also walked to hunt deer and moose and forage for blueberries, sweetgrass, wild tobacco, birch bark, and other food and materials. Surely they paused at the same scenic overlooks and viewpoints as visitors do today. What they thought of the Dawnland view can only be guessed.

Later, European settlers used the "Indian trails"—many are now roads—and created more dirt paths along easy grades: from Beech Mountain down the ridge west of Southwest Harbor to the Seawall; from Norwoods Cove in Southwest Harbor through the notch of Western Mountain, and five or six miles to the northwest arm of Long Pond; Breakneck Road and Route 233; Schooner Head Road.

Early tourists, including artists and scientists, needed trails to experience all that Acadia had to offer. To reach the sublime viewpoint, or see the marks of glaciers, or watch the sun set through the clouds over the sea, one had to get into the landscape, scramble across rocks, borrow a rowboat to reach a trail on the other side, find the path of least resistance to the top of the mountain. Each bushwhacking pioneer made walking easier for those who followed, clearing passage and marking routes.

Popular spots included Great Head and Newport (Champlain) Mountain, near the Lynams' farm where many artists stayed; direct routes along ridgelines, streams, and valleys; or through saddles to Sargent and Green (Cadillac) Mountains.

By 1867 the framework of the current trail system was established and documented in early guidebooks and articles. Authors described how to get to scenic destinations, making it easier for more people. According to Samuel Adams Drake:

> *As the mountains bar the way to the southern shores, you must often make a long detour to reach a given point, or else commit yourself to the guidance of a deer-path, or the dry bed of some mountain torrent . . . In summer or in autumn, with a little knowledge of woodcraft, a well-adjusted pocket-compass, and a stout staff, it is practicable to enter the hills, and make your way as the red huntsmen were of old accustomed to do.*

Drake ignored the fact that "red huntsmen" continued to use the trails on the island at the time of his writing.

Over the next two decades, well-worn paths to the highest summits were marked with blazes, red arrows, and cairns. Wearing flannel walking skirts and stout shoes, woolen pants and hats, the rusticators spread out through the woods and fields, along the shoreline, and up and down summit routes.

Their social status linked to the number of miles hiked over the course of the summer, ladies and gentlemen walked five, ten, and fifteen miles a day. All their tramping and rocking stressed trails and infrastructure. They picked orchids and other rare flowers, stepped on fragile alpine growth, and wandered onto private property.

Landowners and hotels began to restrict access. Cottagers and local businesses feared the loss of beautiful scenery that was the foundation of their economy.

Walkers reacted by protecting access to trails, through managing and purchasing land. In Bar Harbor, citizens reacted by forming the Bar Harbor Village Improvement Association (BHVIA) in 1881. It was one of many civic organizations throughout New England and the country that improved sidewalks and maintained parks. Only at Acadia, however, did "village improvement" extend to building and tending hundreds of miles of hiking trails.

Members of the Appalachian Mountain Club. ACADIA NATIONAL PARK

The BHVIA initially consisted of summer residents, including George Dorr, who were concerned with the upkeep of the village and adjacent Shore Path. In 1892 they created a committee to focus on paths, clearing and marking trails and improving drainage in swampy areas. Dorr created a committee to focus on bicycle paths.

Northeast Harbor formed a village improvement society in 1897, followed by the Seal Harbor Village Improvement Society (1900) and the Southwest Harbor Village Improvement Association (1914). New trails radiated from villages, connecting downtowns with wild areas. The village associations worked together to address the need for a clearly delineated path network (beyond signs and rock piles). In 1896 the first path map of the island was published by Waldron Bates, Herbert Jaques, and Edward Rand (who had gotten to know the island and cut many trails while surveying plants with the Champlain Society and later for *Flora of Mount Desert Island*). They updated the map every few years as boundaries and trails changed.

In the early 1900s the path committees began building more elaborate trails. Waldron Bates, a Boston lawyer with engineering and design skills, built the Giant Slide, Eagle's Crag, Cadillac Cliffs, and other trails that led to rock formations and geological wonders, like Tilting Rock and Bubble Rock, as well as scenic views. In overseeing some twenty-five miles of trails, Bates placed short flights of slab steps and wrote instructions for signs, pointers, steps, bridges, and an open cairn of his own design: "Build the cairns as shown: two large stones with an opening between in line with the direction of the path, across these one flat stone, and on top of this one long stone in line with the direction of the path. Use large stones and set them firmly in place."

In fog or snow, Bates cairns appear like magic, showing the way forward for a lost or uncertain hiker.

Bates's trails would come to seem simple and rustic compared to the "Memorial Trails" crafted under Superintendent Dorr's direction and Andrew Liscomb's crew of builders and masons, with help from Herbert Jaques, a Boston architect, and physician S. Weir Mitchell.

Sponsored by various residents and named in honor of loved ones, trails wound between boulders, skirted open ledges, and paused for expansive views. They were "wide gestures upon the land," as trail crew leader Christian Barter would describe them.

The walking surface was almost entirely constructed, except for areas of ledge or gravel on summits. They used larger stones, with more cuts, as edging or "coping," retaining walls, flat stone "pavement," and tightly fitted steps, sometimes secured with iron pins and staples. The steps served to break up the flow of water, lessen the grade, and protect the trails from erosion. Acadia was the country's first recreational trail system to incorporate extensive use of stone staircases, as seen on the Homans Path, named after Eliza Homans, who was the first to donate land that became

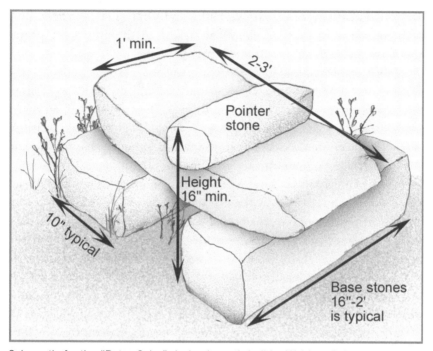

Schematic for the "Bates Cairn" design by path builder Waldron Bates. BALDYGA/
BARTER/ACADIA NATIONAL PARK

part of Acadia National Park. On the Emery Path, more than 670 steps
cut through mazelike walls of towering rock.

Iron rungs, rails, ladders, and bridges appear on a few of Acadia's
trails, especially on the eastern side of Champlain Mountain, where two
prolific path builders, Herbert Jaques and Rudolph Brunnow, had shore-
front homes at the foot of the mountain. In her cultural assessment of
Acadia's trails, Margaret Brown reported that ironwork made it possible
for hikers to climb "in areas that would otherwise require technical rock
climbing gear, or sheer madness."

On the western side of Somes Sound, Walter Buell led design and
construction of the St. Sauveur, Acadia, Beech Mountain, and Western
Mountain trails.

Rudolph Brunnow, a professor of Semitic texts at Princeton, created
technical climbs with iron ladders, railings, and stone steps. While today

the Beehive, Precipice or "Alpine Path," and Orange & Black trails are some of the most popular ascents at Acadia, at the time some people thought they were too constructed, even invasive.

With an expanding trail network, walkers needed guidance. The 1915 *Path Guide of Mount Desert Island* had trail-by-trail descriptions and a revised version of the Rand path map. The guide described routes along mountains and waters that new visitors might overlook, and it also included advice such as "Walks in the woods are enjoyable in fogs and light rains, being more protected than the open roads" and "The beauties of the excursions can be fully enjoyed only when ample time is given for stops on open hill tops or by the brooks."

Aware of the tenuous situation of walking across private property, the guide encouraged hikers to observe fire control laws and avoid littering and "uprooting of plants, barking of trees, and doing injury of any kind."

⁓

After 1913, walkers traveling the route of the old Wabanaki portage along Jordan Stream encountered new gravel carriage roads built by John D. Rockefeller Jr. The roads radiated from his Seal Harbor estate and eventually covered some fifty-seven miles, connecting the northern and southern sections of the park. Reserved for pedestrians, horses, carriages, and bicycles, with places to pause and take in the surroundings, the carriage roads were part of Rockefeller's effort to make available to the public—especially those unable to hike steep or narrow footpaths—more views and scenery, a chance to experience the Divine.

Automobiles—which fueled the growth of the family fortune that enabled Rockefeller to amass great swaths of island property later given to the park for use by the American public—were banned. Surfaced in crushed stone and lined with coping stones of granite block ("Rockefeller's teeth"), the carriage roads wound around mountains and along lakes and ponds. Sixteen unique arched stone bridges crossed over streams, waterfalls, and valleys. The carriage roads enabled new hiking loops and routes, and added to the variety of walking adventures.

The trail builders, including Dorr and Rockefeller, and members of the village improvement societies advocated for land conservation.

When the Hancock County Trustees of Public Reservations formed in 1901, they had a readymade constituency of locals and summer residents who, because of the trails, were familiar with and attached to the Acadia landscape and supported the Trustees' efforts to protect the land. Some also viewed the trails as important to developing the region's economy. As Trustees founder Charles W. Eliot noted, the trails constituted "an important security for the continued prosperity of the island."

The path committees continued their work after the national park was established, on trails both within and outside the park boundary, creating walking and biking paths between villages and nearby nature, expanding the trail network to more than two hundred miles of marked and maintained paths. Village improvement society members kept busy with trail maintenance, adding steps and bridges, fixing retaining walls and drainage, securing handrails, and replacing signs.

The National Park Service, without funds or staff for maintenance, welcomed the help, as the trails remained popular throughout the 1920s. Charles W. Eliot's grandson Charles W. Eliot II wrote, "If there are those who suppose that walking at Mount Desert is a thing of the past, I can testify to the contrary. On one morning last September I met over twenty people on one trail on Sargent Mountain. They were scattered in groups of two or four and ranged in age from 12 to 40 years. The trails are used."

Used as they were, the trails eroded and decayed. Some were rebuilt in the 1930s by the thousands of young men employed by the Civilian Conservation Corps and other Depression-era relief programs. Administrators at Acadia, among the first to apply for CCC crews, welcomed the help. Based at camps near McFarland Hill and Long Pond on Mount Desert Island and in Ellsworth, CCC workers built eighteen miles of new trails, including the Anemone Cave and Long Pond trails, and trails associated with new parking lots, roads, picnic areas, swimming beaches, and campgrounds, according to Park Service "master plans."

CCC crews constructed the one-mile Perpendicular Trail up Mansell Mountain in 1934, one of few complete trails added to the park during the Depression. They built nearly one thousand stone steps secured with retaining walls and discrete pins and cut switchbacks through talus slopes. They quarried natural stone into uniform size and shape to make

Civilian Conservation Corps workers, ca. 1934. ACADIA NATIONAL PARK

consistent treads and spaced risers at a comfortable distance. The crews included local quarry workers laid off during the Depression.

While elsewhere such extensive and obvious staircases might seem too "human" for a wilderness hiking trail, at Acadia steps were often designed and meant to be emphasized as an important aesthetic feature of the trail, blurring the perceived divide between what is "human" and what is "natural." By quarrying native stone from adjacent rocks and moving it painstakingly into place according to site-specific blueprints, path builders revealed the granite foundations of Acadia while enhancing the act of walking and creating erosion-resistant trails. Such highly crafted yet harmonious steps would come to be considered "fundamental" to the experience of hiking at Acadia.

Depression-era trails were designed so hikers with varying levels of ability could access Acadia's beauty. Each trail was to have "an ultimate objective point climaxing the hike" and a natural change of pace from steep climbs to soft, level walks. Though wider than earlier trails, Perpendicular and other CCC paths maintained the tradition of quality and craftsmanship instilled by the early path builders. In contrast to the out-and-back village trails, CCC trails incorporated networks and loops. In buildings, such as the visitor center at Thunder Hole, they used a "rustic style" promoted and popularized by the National Park Service, an approach to architecture and design that incorporated natural materials such as logs and branches, wood shingles, stone, and native plants and animals.

Trail and road work included forestry operations, clearing vegetation, and opening up views at Mount Desert and Schoodic. Workers updated 780 trail signs, using Dorr's renaming scheme. Downhill ski trails on the northwest slope of Sargent Mountain and the south face of Western Mountain were initiated in 1935 but never completed. Landscape architects Benjamin Breeze and George Gordon assisted the crews, with strict guidelines about training, quality construction standards, and reporting requirements.

Despite their good work, with so many trails and an emphasis on "recreation" infrastructure such as picnic areas, much of the CCC work helped to separate the park from the surrounding villages and connector trails. Maintenance needs began to mount. When A. Fitz Roy Anderson took over as cochair of the BHVIA Path Committee in 1937, he noted with concern the poor condition of many trails, a concern voiced by later leaders.

And while park visitation continued to increase, interest in hiking did not. It was no longer in vogue for young people to flirt among the rocks or go on walking dates along the trails. Cars became the preferred way to experience nature, whether driving along the Loop Road or pulling into a campsite.

Hiking barely made it among the top "things you should do in Acadia" listed in the 1941 Bar Harbor's visitor guide:

*1. Take advantage of the free government Nature-Guide Service.
It is for you. Ask for a copy of the printed program.
2. Enjoy the sunset from the top of Cadillac Mountain.*

3. Join the free auto caravan, or drive yourself past Thunder Hole, Otter Cliffs, and on to Northeast Harbor and along the Sargent Drive.
4. Drive to Southwest Harbor.
5. Visit Anemone Cave ("park your car at the parking area").
6. Climb some mountain.

Those who did hike stayed on trails mapped within park boundaries and connected to parking areas. Local residents and longtime summer families continued to use the village paths, but aging village improvement society and association members had a harder time maintaining trails, and many paths, including the Homans Path, began to disappear from maps and guidebooks.

The 1947 fire transformed the eastern side of Mount Desert Island and redirected people's attention. Park maintenance crews began to rebuild popular trails in the 1950s, but few people wanted to hike through the ashes and soot of the burned area. The Park Service closed trails that were seldom used, in poor condition, ran parallel to other paths, or led walkers onto private land. Other trails continued to deteriorate, and Acadia was one of many national parks whose sorry state prompted the Mission 66 initiative of the 1950s and '60s.

———

Named for an American sailor who entered the harbor on the southwestern shore of Mount Desert Island to hide from the British during the Revolutionary War and got stuck in the mud, Ship Harbor became part of the park in 1937. Mission 66 funding enabled construction of a mile-and-a-half looping figure eight of wide, gravel tread along the shoreline and through coastal forest on the eastern side of the harbor. Fourteen numbered posts and a brochure explained the natural and cultural history of the area (glaciers, trees, lichens, tides, shipwrecks).

Short, easy, scenic Mission 66 trails like Ship Harbor were planned on paper first and designed for "enjoyment-without-impairment." The Beech Mountain Summit Loop, accessed via the nearby parking lot, offered mountain scenery and stellar views of Somes Sound without an eight-hundred-foot climb.

At Anemone Cave, Mission 66 funding supported a large parking area and one-way loop, developed to showcase the richly varied life of the sea. Where the CCC constructed a trail that blended in with the surrounding forest, Mission 66 crews paved a wide strip, a clear separation between humans and nature, more about the destination than the route.

Without the investment and manpower of the New Deal, the Mission 66 work was inferior to previous craftsmanship, and much of it fell into disrepair. Trails were closed or neglected. Yet, though the old traditional paths were unmarked, unmapped, and unmaintained, locals continued to use them, creating patterns confusing to visiting hikers.

More outside organizations took an interest in Acadia's trails. The Appalachian Mountain Club (AMC) printed a hiking map of the island in the 1960s, as part of the first Maine Mountain Guide.

The AMC had been leading organized hikes and rock-climbing excursions to Mount Desert Island since the late 1800s. In 1922 AMC members went to the park to camp on the shores of Echo Lake and found that all the thrills of mountain climbing could be had "without the unduly prolonged exertion found elsewhere." For sixty dollars, families could travel from Boston and spend two weeks in tent cabins, taking meals in a dining hall with a stone fireplace, running water, electricity, and telephone lines. "The tired will find opportunity for short walks, water sports, and rest; the sea-lover can indulge in sea-bathing and sailing; the tramper will find beautiful trails and the thrills of real mountain climbs on the slopes and rocky summits of the mountains of the island; all will enjoy the coolness, the invigorating air, the unrivalled views," advertised the *AMC Bulletin* in 1923. In 1925 the camp became permanent, and the AMC acquired the parcel in 1934.

The AMC published a pocket guide to Acadia with a folded map in the 1970s, when the club began helping with trail work. But the resurrection of Acadia's trails awaited the arrival of Gary Stellpflug as the first full-time trail worker in the summer of 1974.

Few and unskilled seasonal crews forced Stellpflug to emphasize stabilizing trails over historical accuracy. He introduced bog boardwalks, log cribbing, and other features to get as many trails in working order as possible. Sections of trail were rerouted. Throughout this work, however, Stellpflug paid attention to unique construction aspects like stone and log water bars, asking himself, "Why does this technique, this placement, this route work?" He located old trails and studied their craft: remnants of granite quarrying twenty or forty feet into the woods, drill holes where rock was split along the grain, radiating stars where dynamite shattered rock, pins that held steps in place, staples that kept slabs of rock from falling. He found magic in uncovering old trails, or things on an existing trail that he'd never noticed before, or figuring out how something was done.

In 1981, under the National Trail System Act of 1968, the secretary of the interior designated the Emery Path, Schiff Path, Kane Path, Kurt's Climb, and Ladder Trail as National Recreation Trails, "exemplary trails of local and regional significance." But throughout the 1980s, Stellpflug and his crews could not keep up with maintenance needs. Nearly three-quarters of all park visitors used the trails; foot traffic was especially heavy on trails near water or ascending mountains. On a typical July or August day, as many as five thousand hikers could be dispersed throughout the park.

The carriage roads deteriorated, too, after Rockefeller's death in 1960 left the park with a huge gap in its maintenance budget. Leaves and other debris clogged culverts, causing flooding and washing away the carriage road surface. Trees and shrubs grew in along the edges, narrowing the roads. As the carriage roads became impassible, they received less attention from the public and were allocated fewer maintenance resources.

On a ranger-led hike through the park in 1985, a group of volunteers got to talking about the state of Acadia's trails and the park's need for support. They had heard about other "Friends" groups throughout the country. They knew the park made decisions that affected the local communities, who at the time had no voice in such matters. They knew that, given people's overwhelming love for Acadia, they had a good chance for success.

Over the course of the following winter, one of the volunteers, Marianne Edwards, worked with park staff to figure out what a new organization would look like. They didn't want to create an advocacy group that pushed the park, but an entity that would act as a bridge between the park and neighboring towns, organize volunteers, and increase funding for the park. In 1986 they established Friends of Acadia.

Within a few years the group had raised the funds to restore the light in the Bear Island Lighthouse and created an eight-million-dollar plan to reconstruct and maintain the carriage roads, with help from Wildwood Stables' Ed Winterburg. They then turned to the hiking trails. If Friends of Acadia could restore the carriage roads, they thought, why not the footpaths, too?

The 1992 General Management Plan for Acadia National Park highlighted rehabilitating and maintaining the hiking trail system as a major goal. Trail maintenance staff increased from one to five. And the park began to seriously evaluate the entire trail system.

Finding a precedent in the old relationship with the village improvement societies, the park sought more help from Friends of Acadia. In 1999 they launched Acadia Trails Forever. The park committed four million dollars, mostly from entry fees, and Friends of Acadia pledged to match it with nine million dollars in private donations. By the end of the year, they had received nearly eight million dollars, including a single five-million-dollar gift, at the time the largest-ever donation to a Maine conservation nonprofit.

Friends of Acadia funded the Acadia Youth Conservation Corps trail rehabilitation program, employing local teens under adult crew leaders for the summer. They worked with the park and Bar Harbor and Southwest Harbor communities to develop connector trails, while reopening four historic trails.

To inform the hiking trails project, the National Park Service collected input from staff and the public through focus groups and workshops. Gary Stellpflug and trail crew leader (and poet) Christian Barter hiked 169 trails and rated each according to cultural resource value,

The early "memorial trails" featured grand gestures to guide walkers through geological features. C. SCHMITT

effects on natural resources and local communities, and the visitor experience. Stellpflug summarized his evaluation:

On eleven specific historic trails at twenty sites, a lack of maintenance, coupled with higher visitor use, has led to collapsing stone stairs, stone culverts, retaining walls, stone paving, coping stones, and loss of the cultural character of these trails, and to trailside natural resource damage. What were once paved walkways, monumental steps, or magnificent retaining walls have become difficult to hike, with loose gravel, slippery and loose stones and steps, exposed roots, and the sad appearance of miserably maintained features. Many steps have been dislodged by ice or as a result of poor maintenance and crumbling of their supporting walls. Drainage structures have collapsed and exacerbated the erosion issues. Trailside soils and vegetation are adversely impacted as hikers seek stable footing away from the deteriorating constructed pathways causing undesirable impacts along trailsides such as nutrification and siltation of nearby streams and dieback of vegetation. Due to the loose stones, the unsightly tread, and the tripping hazards, portions of these trails are unsafe and are very difficult to hike.

The resulting Hiking Trails Management Plan outlined the way forward. Eight miles of abandoned trails would be "rehabilitated," their historic character preserved. In their vision for the trail network, the surviving historic structure and design of the trails commemorated those who designed and built them. Part of this preservation meant no new or expanded parking areas. They accepted that many local residents used abandoned trails and wanted the opportunity to discover old trails, but the park would discourage maintenance of old trails to avoid confusing tourists.

Some trails were reconstructed from scratch, while others needed only to be stabilized. Traditional trail names were recovered. Stellpflug and his crews would repair or replace collapsed culverts, fix 383 stone steps and 355 square feet of retaining wall, replace 50 step stones, and revegetate and stabilize eroded areas. "Restoring crucial historic trails to

Christian Barter, Acadia
National Park trail crew leader.
ACADIA NATIONAL PARK

their proper routes, configurations, and character," Stellpflug wrote, "will
enable visitors to hike trails while enjoying the beauty of these late nineteenth century footpaths."

Each project was carefully planned, mostly in the winter. Any partic-
ular trail rehabilitation cost between twenty thousand and three hundred
thousand dollars in materials and labor.

Every spring, Stellpflug and Barter hiked each trail, looking for
safety issues and following up on feedback about blown-down trees, poor
drainage, and loose steps. Barter, tall and strong from the physical work
of moving stone and earth, kept his senses heightened for poetic potential. Stellpflug, with his shoulder-length white hair and white mustache,
quick wit, and long stride, cast a mystical glow. Together, they created a
vision for Acadia's trail system.

Gary Stellpflug, Acadia National Park trails foreman. ACADIA NATIONAL PARK

In early spring, when the seasonal workers and the student conservation corps came back to work, they began the repairs, one stone step each day. They replaced stones that had been moved by ice and re-cleared old overlooks. Old photographs helped guide restoration. At Sieur de Monts, Stellpflug replaced stepping stones and bridges according to how they appeared in a 1910 image of people gathered at the spring pool. They added more rungs to iron ladders or replaced railings to enhance safety, and widened and graded other trails to modern accessibility standards. Crews began working on another five miles of new trails, including connector paths between the park and villages. In 2003 they cut the ribbon

Jesup Path. C. SCHMITT

on the restored Homans Path, which had been abandoned since the 1940s.

With support from the Friends of Acadia endowment, the trails program went from college kids wandering around cutting brush to a group of professionals with talent and commitment to ensuring that there really will be Acadia trails forever: visionary professionals like Stellpflug, aware of the magic of Acadia's trails, but always hesitant to say more.

The magic is yours. What do you see when you walk here?

Harvest

Making a Living in Acadia

Now the winters drive you crazy
And the fishing's hard and slow.
You're a damn fool if you stay,
But there's no better place to go.
       — FROM THE SONG "THE HILLS OF ISLE AU HAUT"
       BY GORDON BOK

BEGINNING IN THE EIGHTEENTH CENTURY, THE WABANAKI RESIDENTS of Acadia shared space with an increasing number of European colonists, who made their living primarily from the sea, stone, and forest.

Settlers arrived later in Acadia, which was located within contested terrain, fought over by the English and the French in multiple wars between 1678 and 1763. Native Americans fought in these conflicts, usually on the side of the French, to secure protection of their lands from further encroachment by English settlers. They fought on the losing side, and settlers moved in.

In the years surrounding the Revolutionary War, people from the more populated regions of southern New England migrated to the "frontier" of eastern Maine in search of inexpensive and abundant land. Much of the property was, in fact, already claimed.

The British government "granted" large tracts of stolen Wabanaki territory to for-profit proprietors and loyalists, men who had exploited political connections to secure property. Francis Bernard, governor of the Massachusetts colony, was one such grantee. When he arrived on Mount

Desert in 1764, he found that Abraham Somes and John Richardson were already living on the land and had altered the landscape with paths that led to salt marshes, haycocks, fish flakes, and log cabins. Bernard mortgaged his half of Mount Desert to the London merchant banking firm of Lane, Son & Frazer and returned to England.

At Schoodic Point, the same firm may have sent to occupy their vacant holdings an African-American man named Thomas Frazer. The story of Thomas Frazer is intriguing but incomplete. Here are the pieces.

Listed as a "mulatto" with a wife and seven children in the 1790 federal census, Frazer (whose name also appears as Fraser and Frazier) lived in the Schoodic region at least since 1776, when he sold property off Taunton Bay at Egypt Stream. He and his new wife, Mary (described by some sources as Native American), then moved nearby to a hundred-acre homestead lot on the east side of Kilkenny Stream at the head of the Skillings River. They may have lived there until 1799, when Frazer sold the lot, and then moved to the lower harbor on the western side of the Schoodic Peninsula.

Where Frazer came from is unknown. He was a freeman by the time he lived at Schoodic. Was he previously a slave? Frazer could have escaped slavery and/or gained freedom by demonstrating seamanship skills, which are suggested by his waterfront homesites and fisheries-related occupations. At the time a significant percentage of American mariners were of African descent. Frazer could have sailed the West Indies trade triangle and encountered the merchant Thomas Frazer, who was also a sea captain. Was the African-American man a translator, pirate, or whaler, or did he have some other talent that saved him from a life of slavery and sent him to settle in Acadia under the name of his investor?

Historian Allen Workman posits that Frazer was some kind of "agent" for the London merchants Lane, Son & Frazer, who owned the Lower Harbor property in 1792.

It makes sense that the African-American man could have taken the same name as his bosses; according to Bowdoin College professor emeritus Randy Stakeman, it is difficult to trace the former slaves who stayed in Maine and made a new life for themselves because one of a freed slave's first acts was usually to change his or her name.

Having finally located a suitable business site, Frazer started some kind of salt- and fish-processing operation and may have built a tidally powered sawmill on the creek emptying into the harbor. With the exception of what went immediately to the dinner table, all fish was preserved with salt at the time, which turned it into a valuable and nutritious commodity with a long shelf life. According to Workman, with four bushels of salt needed for each barrel of fish, Frazer could not have produced such a volume of salt locally, so he must have imported large volumes of crude rock salt, then refined it by dissolving it in seawater and re-drying. Around the same time, London Atus, another free African-American man who originally came to Machias as a slave, was also involved in salt production and sea trade.

Archaeologists working at the Frazer homestead dug up coarse and refined redware, pearlware, creamware, dark green bottle glass, window glass, cut and hand-forged nails, brick, a copper button, a broken brass shoe buckle, a white-clay tobacco pipe stem, an eighteenth-century pewter rattail spoon, an early nineteenth-century handblown wine bottle, and an 1802 US penny. Animal bones uncovered show the Frazer family kept cows, pigs, sheep, and chickens, and hunted or trapped white-tailed deer and the now-extinct sea mink.

Frazer and his family remained at the harbor into the first decades of the nineteenth century, even after the colonial proprietors sold their interests in the land to William Bingham agent David Cobb. Records of Frazer cease after 1820.

It is rumored that Thomas Frazer died while trying to release a load of a neighbor's floating logs one Sunday morning. Writing years after the event, chroniclers variously reported the cause of death as overexertion or drowning.

What crops did Frazer grow? Farming was a tougher go. Most residents of Acadia dug out the rocky soil that had developed in between the mountains and planted rye, wheat, barley, oats, buckwheat, beans, peas, turnips, carrots, beets, corn, and potatoes. Described as "sturdy stock," simple, honest, and frugal, early settler families engaged in a diverse way of life demanded by Acadia's changing seasons and harsh winters. Farming occurred alongside fishing, lumbering, shipbuilding, trading,

Objects recovered during archaeological investigations of the Frazer homestead at Schoodic: a "rat-tail" spoon, fish hook, pieces of a milk pan, a clay marble, and an 1802 US coin. ACADIA NATIONAL PARK

or "coasting": trading fish, lumber, and granite for wheat, corn, cotton, sugar, molasses, rum, and salt. Acadia was a small part of a global trading network that included the capture and enslavement of African people; Thomas Frazer's role in this trade, and perceptions of it, can only be speculated.

Like Frazer, the newly arriving settlers chose locations on shore land with access to the sea and running water nearby. They needed salt marshes to provide hay for their livestock. They dammed, ditched, and drained the salt marsh meadows for hay, cultivated cranberries, and planted apple trees. They made butter, honey, maple syrup, and cider. They also raised pigs, cows, chickens, and sheep. The sheep—thousands of them—had a visible influence on the landscape, keeping meadows open and clear.

Early visitors viewed agriculture and other natural-resource-based work as part of the scenic character of Acadia and remarked upon it regularly. William Henry Bishop, writing for *Harper's* in 1885, offered a particularly detailed portrait of Isle au Haut: "Sheep were kept; the principal crops were turnips, hay, and wool. There was an enormous fish as the vane of the meeting-house. The minister had just then suddenly gone insane."

Acadia's geology provided another means to survival, as settlers cut raw material for local building foundations. After the Civil War, increasing demand for granite paralleled the rapid urban expansion along the East Coast. In the late 1800s multiple granite quarries in Acadia, such as the Hall or McMullen Quarry, exported the majority of their product via schooner to major cities for use as foundations, facades, supporting walls, monuments, breakwaters, dry docks, curbs, street paving, bridge abutments, gravestones, and hitching posts. A copper mine on Beech Mountain operated briefly in the 1880s.

Fishing, however, was the primary product for both sustenance and trade in Acadia. The Wabanaki harvested clams, fish, lobsters, ducks, and seals; they hunted porpoise for meat and fat. Europeans caught cod, mostly, but also herring, haddock, hake, cusk, pollock, menhaden, mackerel, alewives, lobsters, and clams; they killed whales for their oil. Salt was important to the fish trade, which is why it is reasonable that Thomas Frazer had some kind of salt operation.

About twenty-five people lived at Schoodic Point in the 1840s. Frazer sold his property to John Frisbee of Portsmouth, who expanded the fish operations and hired local crew to process fish landed by his vessel *Industry*. From the 1840s until 1857, Leonard Holmes was the principal fish-maker of the operation. He eventually sold out to his partner, fishing captain Charles Norris.

Another saltworks was established by Calvin Turner, at Seal Trap on Isle au Haut in 1800. Turner's salt supplied families and neighbors, whose vessels sailed from Penobscot Bay to Grand Manan or fished for cod closer to home. Men of all ages worked the waters; women salted and dried the fish. Here, Bishop again on Isle au Haut:

> *An occasional tide-mill, turned each way by ebb and flow, is found on these deep coves. The grist from them is said to be of a better quality than from the steam-mills, being less heated in the process. But the coves are much more turned to account as natural traps for fish. Weirs of sticks and brush, with a single entrance left, are set across them, and the entrance is closed at high tide, imprisoning whatever has passed in. The bottom is almost bare at low water. [We] heard of famous catches of mackerel, shad, and black-fish, which had been headed off and driven in by a cordon of boats, and stranded on the mud when the tide had gone out. One of [our] informants said he had thus made fifty dollars in a single day.*

In the middle of the nineteenth century, when the first tourists arrived to draw and study and write about the region's natural scenery, they moved through a landscape inhabited by indigenous people with thousands of years of culture and traditions, and a place transformed by the descendants of European settlers and their industry. The Wabanaki continued their traditional seasonal practices on Mount Desert and surrounding islands: collecting sweetgrass in the marshes, hunting moose in the autumn woods, trapping eels and alewives in the streams, digging clams from the cold mud. And thousands of residents were busy tending farms, woodlots, and fishing weirs.

Early tourists admired the open hillsides grazed by sheep, and wooden cabins tucked into the valleys. Such pastoral views contributed to their idea of the "picturesque." They looked upon the Indians with curiosity, sympathy, and an attitude of superiority. Shipwrecks, like the one in the old painting by Thomas Doughty, reappeared in published sketches, throwbacks to a more romantic time.

But it was perhaps inevitable that the visitors, whose numbers were increasing, would come into conflict with the local residents. The wilderness experience they expected was interrupted by the activity of daily life and commerce: the noise of quarrying, the messy roadsides, and the smell of rotting fish.

Though occasionally picturesque, lobster factories began to garner complaints. Such plants existed in Southwest Harbor, where the Underwood Company of Boston built a lobster cannery in 1853. Additional canneries followed in Bass Harbor (Underwood), Prospect Harbor (Russell & Co.), Hammond's Cove in South Gouldsboro, and the Isle au Haut Thoroughfare. (Operated by Lewis & Brothers, the Isle au Haut business did not last long. Local fishermen clashed with supervisors over plant management and prices, and some "unpleasantness" resulted in the company moving off the island in 1871.)

By the 1880s the Southwest Harbor cannery employed fifty people to can not only lobster but also clams and clam chowder, fish chowder, mackerel, and salmon. Lobster meat was picked and packed in eight-ounce cans. Lobsters were also boiled whole in the shell and then packed, tail bent, into tall cylindrical cans.

Though men did most of the heavy lifting at the factory, unloading the boats and hauling crates, women and children, with small and nimble hands, did most of the packing. The work was demanding, with no set hours. Workers rushed to the factory whenever the whistle blew. The conditions were dismal. As one anonymous source described them, "The windows were jammed with dampness and years of dirt and grime and could not be opened to allow air to circulate. The women packers had to work all day in the factories and then look after the children and household chores when they went home. The work was dangerous and many children lost fingers on the cutting tables." Later, canneries shifted to packing sardines. The Southwest Harbor plant became Addison Packing Co. and then Stinson's sardine cannery. Camps housed factory workers, including many Wabanaki.

Lobstermen supplied the canneries with fresh, live lobsters, transported in lobster smacks—schooners or small sailboats with water-filled cargo holds. Others built pounds to hold live lobsters before sale or transport—including Civil War veteran Ezra A. Over, another African-American "mulatto" entrepreneur in the history of Schoodic.

One of seven children of Henry and Nancy Over (or Ober), Ezra was born around 1850 and grew up in Steuben. He had been working as a fisherman and transported lobsters to the Prospect Harbor cannery. In 1875 he bought Schoodic Island, where he stored the local lobster catch. For a year or two, he and his wife, Abbie Jane Huckins, stayed with her family at nearby Wonsqueak Harbor to oversee the island operation, both for factory supply and the fresh lobster tourist market in Bar Harbor. In 1896 Over began building the first lobster pound in the region at Bunkers Harbor, operated with his father-in-law, Frank Huckins, for several decades.

Wilson "Wid" Sargent and Elisha Bridges built another lobster pound at Thomas Frazer's old property at Lower Harbor in 1924.

For those who still harvested cod and other fish, catching and processing their catch required shoreside infrastructure, a need that gave rise to dozens of "fish houses," or "fish shacks," lining the shores of Acadia. Some had smokehouses and docks, others just a small beach or shoal where boats could land. Rustic structures assembled from driftwood and scavenged materials, fish houses were used for storing and preparing gear, holding and curing bait, drying and processing fish. They were places to access the water, the interface between work at sea and on land. And, at the beginning or end of the day, or during winter, some fish houses provided space where fishermen gathered and built traps, mended nets, painted buoys, and baited hooks. Inside the fish house, fishermen exchanged knowledge, obscene jokes, and coarse truths.

Two men pulling nets from their fishing dory, 1890. H. L. RAND / #5335 THE SOUTHWEST HARBOR PUBLIC LIBRARY COLLECTION OF PHOTOGRAPHS

Fishing weirs—fenced, mazelike enclosures of sticks, brush, netting, and line—trapped migrations of Atlantic herring and other fish. Rodick's weir at Bar Island was especially efficient, trapping tens of thousands of pounds of fish in a single turn of the tide. Herring were trapped at Moore's Harbor on Isle au Haut, Schoodic's Lower Harbor, Baker Island, and all around the coves and islands of Acadia. At Arey Cove on Schoodic's Little Moose Island, six Coombs brothers kept a family summer base camp and fish house to be near their traps and nets.

Most of the catch was salted and dried on shore, and the rest was pickled or smoked and shipped to New York and other eastern cities. Around 1900 about seventy men worked at fish-drying stations around Frenchman Bay, splitting fish and laying them out to dry in the sun on fish flakes (drying racks) along the shore or even on rooftops. Plenty of fishing families refused to yield to the pressure of the tourist industry and continued to cure their fish and take part in the coasting trade.

Quaker tourists who visited Mount Desert in 1865 toured the lobster cannery. The guests along on *The Cruise of the Forest Home* reported:

This institution was a novelty to all of us, very few of our party having even so much as heard of the existence of such a branch of industry. The building was a large two-story brick structure, standing partly over the water. Within its walls two thousand five hundred unhappy Crustacians [sic] were daily boiled to death, and their remains, after being taken from the shell, packed away in air-tight tin cans and carried to Boston."

Many viewed the tourism industry as a positive influence on Acadia's year-round community, as captured by historian George Street:

It was certainly at a fortunate time for the Mount Desert people that the summer business began. The local occupations were declining, and no new industries, like the granite business which developed later, had appeared to help solve the problem of making a living. The herring fisheries were becoming less and less profitable, the coasting trade was slack, the hills had been stripped of the last trees suitable for sawing, the thin soil of the farms was practically exhausted. With the coming of the new population that arrived with the roses and disappeared with the first frosts, the whole aspect of affairs changed. The summer business meant for the people of the island towns an outward prosperity such as they had never imagined.

At first, tourist complaints of the sights and smells of fishing did little harm to the fishing business, at least compared to the damage inflicted by industry.

Logging and associated dam construction harmed populations of migratory river fishes like alewives, a prime food source for cod. The fishing industry harmed itself, too: Menhaden, another cod prey item, also were depleted by fish oil factories in the region. In response to resulting declines in coastal cod populations, fishermen "diversified," targeting other species like haddock, hake, pollock, cusk, tuna, swordfish, and halibut. In 1887, 726 fishermen worked 46 vessels and 439 boats. They caught fish with gill nets, purse seines, haul seines, weirs, fyke nets, and 12,900 lobster traps.

By the mid-century, new technology in the form of petroleum-powered, bottom-trawling, and gill-netting vessels and refrigeration accelerated the decline. On Isle au Haut, the number of working fishermen had dropped from more than sixty in 1870 to twenty-five in 1930, although fishing remained the dominant occupation.

Other industries were affected by the fire of 1947, which destroyed many buildings. The forest, later turned into a park, reclaimed many of the homesteads and farms of Acadia; the rising sea eroded Wabanaki shell middens. In some cases the National Park Service tore down homes, only to regret decades later the lost historic value of such "cultural resources." Amid the spruce and fir, the former residents of Acadia live on in lilacs, apple trees, and wide-crowned maples, crumbling stone walls, granite benches, garden hedges, and cellar holes.

———

Of all the harvest in Acadia, logging had the greatest impact on the landscape and the park. More than fishing, the logging industry riled the tourists, and prompted calls for conservation of Acadia's diverse ecosystems.

Abraham Somes built the first dam and mill in Acadia, at the head of the sound on Mount Desert, which sprawled into a complex of bark mill, sawmill, shingle mill, gristmill, two shipyards, and a tanyard. The new residents dammed nearly every freshwater stream and lake outlet to power saw blades. John Peters's 1794 map of Mount Desert Island showed sawmills at Somes Sound, Bar Harbor, and Seal Cove. Logs covered the surface of lakes and harbors; on shore, stacked lumber awaited shipment.

In some cases, as on Mill Creek in Winter Harbor, they built mills before houses or other settlements and exported the timber by sea. At Schoodic, where fewer people lived, the forests were logged hard and early, the timber shipped to feed the lime works at Rockland. The kilns consumed wood continuously, and loggers cut wherever boats could be

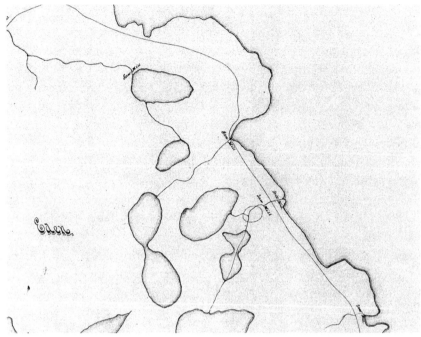

Excerpt from the 1794 Peters map of Mount Desert Island, showing sawmills on Bar Harbor streams (Duck Brook, Eddie Brook, Witch Hole Ponds, etc.).
ACADIA NATIONAL PARK

brought near shore and loaded with wood. Anything that would burn was logged.

Logging was not extensive on Isle au Haut, with limited mill activity at Head Harbor and nearby Thurlow's Island. On Mount Desert Island, loggers and mill operators went about their business without much challenge throughout the first half of the nineteenth century. At first, cutting was selective, allowing softwoods to regenerate in the understory, and the mills seemed to fit the landscape.

Augustus Savage remembered the seasonal nature of woods work by his father and uncle in the early 1800s: "They both went coasting and fishing in the summer and in winter they hauled out logs and cord wood to sell in western markets. They cut and hewed frames for their houses,

Higgins sawmill at Somes Sound, Mount Desert, Maine, 1890. H. L. RAND / #5122 THE
SOUTHWEST HARBOR PUBLIC LIBRARY COLLECTION OF PHOTOGRAPHS

rafted logs to Somesville for the boarding, sawed and shaved pine shingles for their houses and barns."

Brothers George and John Jordan acquired a sawmill at the outlet of one of the large ponds in 1839 and began harvesting timber from the surrounding hillsides, hauling logs along a dirt road to the beach at Seal Harbor. They built a house and planted an apple orchard on the southern shore. The house later became a tearoom serving the public: the Jordan Pond House.

Just as early tourists appreciated agricultural activities like sheep grazing, they viewed lumber mills as "scenic." Clara Barnes Martin noted the mill in the Great Meadow in her guidebook, and an abandoned mill at Duck Brook became a favorite subject of photographers. By 1870 there were two steam sawmills, one at Salisbury Cove and the other at Pretty Marsh, and ten water sawmills.

According to historian Richard Judd, the situation changed with the arrival of the paper industry and the portable sawmill in the 1880s. The new saws could be moved from place to place wherever loggers could find a tract of sufficient size to justify setting up. The portable sawmill made it possible and profitable to cut timber in places that previously had been inaccessible. According to Judd, rapid expansion of the logging industry, mechanization, and intensive cutting triggered a strong sense of unease.

Tourists, summer visitors, scientists, and local residents began to take note of the cutting. More people walking through the woods meant more people would notice harvesting activity, and protest anything that interfered with their experience of Acadia. Their criticisms of how the locals treated the land reveal an enduring tension between year-round, generational residents of Acadia and those "from away."

In her guidebook, Martin wrote, "Except in one or two almost inaccessible valleys, the forest primeval is all gone; but huge stumps and scathed trunks show what the axe and the fires have done." And Drake's *Nooks and Corners* noted second-growth forests: "The poverty or greed of the inhabitants has sacrificed every tree that was worth the labor of felling."

In 1889 Champlain Society member and Botanical Department chair Edward Rand wrote in *Garden and Forest*:

The forests of Mount Desert Island were once full of wealth, and full of wealth they still would be if the lumbermen and the forest-fire had not done their work so well. The first permanent settlement on the island was founded on the lumber business, which drags out a slow existence there to-day . . . High up on the mountains, through the mountain gorges, along the ponds, everywhere, the great trees growing on the thin but rich wood-soil were taken out, not one by one, but all together, and the forest-fire followed. To-day nearly every saw-mill is in ruins; the mountains are bare; acres upon acres are overgrown only with a poor wood-growth that years will bring to little or nothing; the soil has been burned off or washed away; the streams preserve no even flow. There is no longer much to fear from lumbering, but two saw-mills at Somesville are still doing infinite harm to the beautiful

Great Pond Woods, and should [be] stopped without delay. If the town of Mount Desert values its attractions as a summer resort, it could well afford to purchase and destroy both these mills . . .

This great reason for jealously preserving the remaining woods of Mount Desert Island is their infinite value as a part of the wild scenery of the place, and their wonderful attraction to the city-wearied man or woman in search of a summer home and resting-place. With the destruction of the forest-beauty and the impairment of the scenery will come depreciation in land values and diminished attentions as a summer resort.

Rand went on to lament wasteful wood-chopping, the desecration of Hunter's Brook valley, unsightly roadsides, and erection of telegraph wires. "Some resolute policy must be adopted for protecting the forest-scenery of Mount Desert, or it will be robbed of its peculiar charm and be converted into an inhospitable waste," he wrote.

Trail builder Herbert Jaques joined the growing number of people advocating protection of land. In the late summer of 1895, in a letter preserved in the Bar Harbor Village Improvement Association files, Jaques described his attempt to purchase land between Green (Cadillac) and Pickett (Huguenot) Mountains owned by the Rodick family, calling attention to "the great destruction of the forests caused by the cutting of firewood each year" and urging

the importance of acquiring and preserving large tracts of wild land while yet there is still time. For instance the superb birch grove on the way to Sargent's Mountain at the foot of McFarland's Hill and also the woods in the South West Valley which are being rapidly destroyed. In fact the whole country about Eagle Lake and a large portion about Jordan's pond is liable to be destroyed, as far as the woods are concerned. Can we not save this beautiful region both on account of its sanitary as well as its aesthetic value?

Scientists, too, were critical. "Everything down to even three inches at the small end is sawed up," wrote ecologists Barrington Moore and

Norman Taylor. "Obviously this results in utilizing much material which under the older methods was left in the tops to rot in the woods . . . This modern method results in considerable quantities of slash."

⌁

Visitors may have been scrutinizing the actions of the year-round folk, but local residents took equal notice of the wandering tourists, who roamed freely over privately owned land, scrambled through underbrush, walked across open ledges, and rested in hayfields and pastures. Property owners, increasingly concerned with trespassing, began to restrict access and build fences to control livestock and delineate boundaries.

Meanwhile, people had found another way to profit from the land—by selling it to the very tourists who abhorred the destruction of trees, flowers, and other natural features. Speculative land companies aggressively promoted Mount Desert property. Sales of shares in the Bar Harbor Land Company accelerated after the first pass of the Bar Harbor

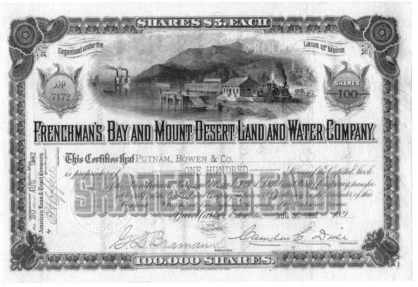

Stock certificate for the Frenchman's Bay and Mount Desert Land and Water Company, 1892. GLABARRE.COM

Express train, which raised land values throughout Acadia and led to a dozen similar real estate speculators.

The Mount Desert and Eastern Shore Land Company advertised five hundred available lots, advising investors to buy now, for the lots would soon increase in price as proposed roads and other improvements made the lands accessible. The company began preparing a map for a real estate development in Seal Harbor. In his 1886 guidebook, W. B. Lapham noted that in Bar Harbor, "Land has advanced in price a thousand fold, and choice building lots will command almost any sum asked."

More people coming to Acadia and loving it. More people making a living from tourists. More people using the trails and traversing the landscape. More people trying to buy up pieces of the landscape for their own personal use and enjoyment. More people seeking to profit from natural resources. More seasonal residents who had formed a deep and lasting attachment to Acadia. More people calling for conservation. At the turn of the twentieth century, these things combined led some people to finally take action to protect Acadia.

Reservation

The Founding of Acadia National Park

*Can nothing be done to preserve for the use and enjoyment of the great
unorganized body of the common people some fine parts, at least, of
this sea-side wilderness of Maine?*
—CHARLES ELIOT, WRITING IN *GARDEN AND FOREST* IN 1890

THE BEEHIVE TOWERS FIVE HUNDRED FEET ABOVE THE OCEAN AT THE
southeastern edge of Acadia National Park on Maine's Mount Desert
Island. The Beehive's mounded, blocky appearance resulted from glaciers
"plucking" away angular pieces of granite. In between the bare rock surface, pitch pine and cedar adorn the ledges, tempting hikers to ascend via
the "Little Precipice" path, a short but invigorating climb with iron rails,
bridges, and ladders. From the summit, one can look down upon waves
tumbling toward the golden beach. The sands of Sand Beach are mostly
eroded, broken shells of marine animals thousands of years old.

To the north, the peaks of Champlain, Dorr, and Cadillac Mountains
are all within sight, and the in-between valleys of spruce and pine, the
Porcupine Islands and Frenchman Bay beyond. In *The Artist's Mount
Desert*, Thomas Cole is quoted on Sand Beach and the Beehive, "This is
a very grand scene—the craggy mountains, the dark pond of dark brown
water—the golden sea sand of the beach and the light green sea with
its surf altogether with the woods of varied color—make a magnificent
effect such as is seldom seen combined in one scene."

Over the summit and down sits the Bowl. Pale gray rocks slope into
clear, dark waters, undisturbed but for a splattering of fragrant water lilies

The Bowl, part of the first parcel of land donated to the Hancock County Trustees of Public Reservations in 1908. The Beehive is the hill on the far side of the pond.
C. SCHMITT

along the edge and silvery driftwood felled by beavers that also helped create the pond. A siphon once carried water from the Bowl to customers of the Beehive Mountain Aqueduct Company; the property itself was owned by Eliza Homans of Boston.

Eliza Homans knew that no one could really "own" a place as strangely beautiful and magical as the Bowl and the Beehive. It was not a place she could keep for herself. In May 1908 the longtime summer resident of Bar Harbor gave the 140 acres surrounding the Bowl and the Beehive to the Hancock County Trustees of Public Reservations: the first large parcel that later became part of Acadia National Park, the gift incited a series of land donations and purchases.

Born Eliza Lee to Mary and Samuel K. Lothrop in Dover, New Hampshire, in 1832, she grew up in Boston, where her father served as Unitarian pastor of the historic Brattle Street Church. She married Charles Dudley Homans in 1856.

The couple lived in Boston's new Back Bay neighborhood; Charles Homans's intense work as a surgeon required equally intense vacations. Charley and Lizzie traveled extensively, including outdoors-oriented excursions to the Adirondacks and more cultured tours of Europe. Since the 1870s they went nearly every summer to their cottage on Oak Hill near Schooner Head. They likely were introduced to Mount Desert Island by Eliza's brother, who jointly purchased property with Charles Hazen Dorr, George Dorr's father.

Eliza Homans outlived her husband, who died of a gallbladder infection at age sixty. Grief could not prevent her from traveling the world, alone, visiting her daughter, who had moved with her husband to India; managing multiple properties in Boston and Maine; or presiding over the first meeting of Boston's Mayflower Club (named after the flower, not the immigrant vessel). She founded the ladies' social club with her sister: a place to foster "female independence of thought and deed," where women could get a meal or a room to sleep. The club rejected intellectual competition or talk of politics; the conservative Lizzie campaigned against voting rights for women, yet her travel diaries suggest she supported her fellow women and seemed interested in the women of the world. She was described as a most remarkable woman of brilliant conversation, always standing erect, well costumed, alert.

More grief came to Eliza Homans when her two children died within one year of each other. Her son died in May 1902 of Bright's disease, and one year later her daughter died from typhoid fever en route to Maine from her home in India.

Homans continued to summer in Acadia, by then a place with deep meaning for her and her family. Her friendship with Charles W. Eliot, likely strengthened by their shared Boston Unitarian roots, combined with her concern for the future of her summer home, prompted her to gift the land. In a letter to Eliot, she recognized that if she did not engage the Trustees in protecting the land, she ran the risk that her grandchildren "may find a 'Merry-Go-Round' established there!"

Eliza Homans. ACADIA NATIONAL PARK

She reserved the right to shoot, fish, boat, and keep a boathouse on the Bowl and specified the Beehive Mountain Aqueduct Company would continue to use the pond to provide water to nearby residents. She put no other restrictions on the deed and wanted the land transfer publicized, but not her name. She also donated to the Maine Sea Coast Mission; she gave a complete set of the Official Records of the Civil War to the Bar Harbor library, and requested that any money not inherited go to Harvard to establish a professorship in honor of her husband.

Charles W. Eliot shared Homans's grief of loss. His first wife had died young, and his son Charles died of spinal meningitis at the age of thirty-seven. At the time of his death, Charles Eliot was working with Frederick Law Olmsted, having left his own landscape architecture business to join the Olmsted firm as partner. In his short career, the young Eliot had transformed an unregulated district of rail yards, shantytowns, and factories in Revere, Massachusetts, into the first public beach in America. Designing a park along the Charles River from Cambridge to Watertown, he also worked on plans for an Emerald Necklace of parks surrounding the city.

Fortified by his youthful experiences of camping and sailing around Acadia and continued engagement with the Maine landscape as a professional, Charles Eliot knew the place better than most other gardeners and architects. He wrote in his journal in 1883–84, "The scenery of Mount Desert is so beautiful and remarkable that no pains should be spared to save it from injury—to the end that many generations may receive all possible benefit and enjoyment from the sight of it."

Charles Eliot viewed public parks and squares as necessities of modern town life, lands that should be set aside for the public, for recreation, fresh air, quiet, and contemplating scenery. In his landscape architecture practice, he sought to preserve everything that was distinctive, "to create as much as possible of beauty." He thought industry and human history contributed to the scenery and should be highlighted rather than erased. The landscape architect was critical of people who tried to re-create the European aesthetic on the Maine coast, by converting lichen-covered rocks, dwarf pines and spruces, and thickets of sweet fern, bayberry, and wild rose to lawns.

"The English park, with its great trees and velvet turf, is supremely beautiful in England, where it is simply the natural scenery perfected; but save in those favored parts of North America where the natural conditions are approximately those of the Old Country, the beauty of it cannot be had and should not be attempted," he wrote in one of many articles for *Garden and Forest*. Instead, he argued for paying attention to local nature, to "perfecting each type in its own place."

Charles William Eliot, cofounder of Acadia National Park. ACADIA NATIONAL PARK

Throughout the 1880s and 1890s, he corresponded with fellow Champlain Society member Edward Rand and others about ways to protect Mount Desert Island and the greater Boston area. In 1891 he conceived and helped create The Trustees of Public Reservations in Massachusetts, the first private land trust in the world. He died six years later.

Charles W. Eliot revisited these accomplishments in the winter of 1900–1901, as he was compiling his deceased son's biography. Going through papers and journals, he reread notes and published articles about the need to protect Mount Desert Island, such as this one from 1890:

The real danger of the present situation is that this annual flood of humanity, with its permanent structures for shelter, may so completely overflow and occupy the limited stretch of coast which it invades, as

to rob it of that flavor of wildness and remoteness which hitherto has hung about it, and which in great measure constitutes its refreshing charm . . . The readers of Garden and Forest *stand in need of no argument to prove the importance to human happiness of that refreshing antidote to city life which fine natural beauty supplies, nor is it necessary to remind them that love of beauty and of art must surely die if it be cut at its roots by destroying or vulgarizing the beauty of nature . . . The United States have but this one short stretch of Atlantic sea-coast where a pleasant summer climate and real picturesqueness of scenery are to be found together. Can nothing be done to preserve for the use and enjoyment of the great unorganized body of the common people some fine parts, at least, of this sea-side wilderness of Maine?*

Charles Eliot, who inspired the conservation of lands that would become Acadia National Park. *CHARLES ELIOT, LANDSCAPE ARCHITECT*

The mission could not have been more clear. Eliot would finish what his son had started, and secure for all Mount Desert Island's most magnificent scenery, an antidote to modern city life. But he could not, would not, do it alone—only through collective action could such a feat be achieved. He reached out to the village improvement societies, civic associations of local and seasonal residents involved in trail building and maintenance, infrastructure, and beautification of Mount Desert Island village centers.

Each organization sent representatives to a meeting on August 13, 1901, at the Music Room in Seal Harbor. Caroline Dana Bristol had built the one-room structure as a place to practice piano without waking her children from their afternoon naps or disturbing them in the evening after they had gone to bed. Perched on the slope of Ox Hill with a view of the harbor through diamond-paned windows, the Music Room had become a neighborhood gathering spot.

Also in the room was Charles W. Eliot's Boston friend George B. Dorr, who first came to the island with his family at the age of fourteen in 1868. His father, Charles Hazen Dorr, joined Eliza Homans's brother, Thornton Lothrop, in purchasing the Higgins Tract of land at Cromwell Harbor. Dorr later bought Lothrop out and built the Old Farm estate. Since then, George Dorr had expanded his landholdings along Schooner Head Road, Cromwell Harbor Brook, and the Great Meadow. Dorr had brought along railway executive George Vanderbilt and New York banker John S. Kennedy.

They agreed to form the Hancock County Trustees of Public Reservations, Maine's first land trust, modeled after the Massachusetts organization created by the late Charles Eliot. Charles W. Eliot was elected president (a position he held until his death in 1926), Dorr and geology professor Edward S. Dana, vice presidents; George Stebbins, treasurer; and Lea Luquer, secretary.

Filing paperwork to incorporate the following month were the officers and Luere B. Deasy, Edward B. Mears, and Loren E. Kimball. An additional thirty-eight men signed on as members in that first year, including path builders Waldron Bates and Herbert Jaques.

The incorporation was confirmed by a special act of the state legislature in 1903, giving the Trustees power to "acquire, hold and maintain and improve for free public use lands in Hancock County which by reason of scenic beauty, historical interest, sanitary advantage or for other reasons may be available for the purpose." The act also exempted Trustee lands from state, county, or town taxes.

Charles W. Eliot envisioned an island with a summer population of both cottagers and boarders, who shared an interest with year-round residents in protecting Mount Desert Island and developing it the "right" way, as he detailed in a 1904 pamphlet. Together, seasonal and year-round residents would preserve access to the shore, make roads tidy and beautiful, and keep foot trails narrow, rough, and wild. "The whole island ought to be treated by every resident, and by the body of voters, as if it were a public park; that is, the beauty and convenience of the place as a health and pleasure resort ought to be kept constantly in mind to guide the policy of the towns and the habits and customs of the population."

While Eliot avoided using the word "tourism," his words reflected a faith that protected landscapes, designed by architects and controlled and managed by the federal government, would benefit local residents economically. He also echoed the old tension between seasonals and year-rounders, in thinking that island conditions needed to be "improved" with outside help.

Eliot invited local residents to support the Trustees in their efforts to secure large areas of land on the island for free public use, particularly the hilltops, and narrow pieces of shore which lay between public highways and the sea.

Eliza Homans was the first to respond, with her Bowl and Beehive parcel. A few months later, the Cooksey family donated two small lots—a site on Barr Hill overlooking Jordan Pond and a tiny square in Seal Harbor, set aside for a plaque to memorialize the landing of Samuel de Champlain in 1604. Behind the scenes, George Dorr and local attorney Albert H. Lynam identified tracts of land for potential acquisition.

For Dorr, the Trustees provided a mechanism for buying, holding, and protecting land. The land trust allowed him to fulfill his vision. Green

(Cadillac) Mountain, as the tallest height along the East Coast with obvious development appeal, became the next target. Hearing that land speculators intended to purchase the summit, build a road, and possibly subdivide the acreage, Dorr and Kennedy purchased the land from the estate of Daniel W. Brewer in 1908. The Trustees next acquired the east side of Dry (Dorr) Mountain and the Tarn.

As Richard Hale wrote of Dorr, "Whenever a crisis came in the fortunes of the mountains that became the park, it was he who saw to it that something was done. Consequently, to this day, the park reflects his personality."

The Trustees, equally concerned with public health and sanitation in Acadia's villages, early on protected lands that bordered the public water supplies of Eagle and Jordan Ponds.

George Dorr, cofounder and first superintendent of Acadia National Park. ACADIA NATIONAL PARK

The lakes and ponds in Acadia are deep granite basins carved by glaciers, filled with cold, clear water. The Bowl is among the highest in elevation; Jordan Pond is the deepest and clearest; Eagle Lake is among the largest and provided water power at its outlet to Duck Brook. Known as Young's Pond for landowner Ezra Young, and later Great Pond, Eagle Lake began supplying drinking water in 1874, after outbreaks of typhoid and scarlet fevers prompted local hotel owners and summer residents to secure a quality water supply. Acadia's vacationers were well acquainted with urban ills such as sewage and related illnesses, and the last thing they or the local hotel owners wanted was for the same issues to plague their summer idyll.

By the summer of 1875, the private Bar Harbor Water Company, run primarily by the Rodick brothers, had built a mile and a half of open wooden flumes from Duck Brook to a new reservoir. Over the next few years, the company expanded and improved the system and built new dams, reservoirs, distribution pipes, and fire hydrants in an effort to keep up with the village's growth. A massive aqueduct structure spanned the Duck Brook Valley.

Dissatisfaction with management of the water supply system led some summer residents to start their own water company and eventually take over operations from the Rodicks. New directors included Trustee members John S. Kennedy and Fred Lynam.

The lake remained undeveloped, save for an ice-cutting operation and two small hotels: the Lake House near the outlet and the Curran House near the northwest end. Ferryboats transported tourists to the Green (Cadillac) Mountain railroad, but all of the infrastructure was gone by the turn of the century except for an icehouse.

Then, late in 1909, after all the summer residents had left, Philip Livingston of New York began building a camp on the east shore of Eagle Lake. No one took notice until a few months later, when an "enthusiastic" account of the development appeared in the weekly paper, subscribed to by summer residents. Alarmed, and afraid that other cottages were soon to follow, directors of the water company moved to prevent development of Eagle Lake. In the meeting of January 17, 1910, the executive committee discussed not only the desirability of preventing Livingston from building a cottage, but also, for the first time on record, the need to develop a comprehensive plan to safeguard the future purity of Eagle Lake.

They contacted Dorr, who immediately spread word of what was happening. Dr. Robert Abbe, chair of the Bar Harbor Village Improvement Association's sanitary committee, wrote a letter denouncing the project. Abbe told Dorr he could publish the letter if necessary.

With Abbe's letter in hand, Dorr packed his bag and took the night train to Bar Harbor and met with Lynam. Lynam was doubtful anything could be done. With construction so far along, it would cost too much to stop work. But after reading Abbe's concerns, and not wanting to shake public confidence in the drinking water supply, Lynam exclaimed, "For God's sake, don't print that letter!" and then contacted Livingston at his winter home in Florida and convinced him to sell his land for three times what he paid for it.

Lynam agreed to finance the purchase of land the water company wished to protect, but that actual title would be placed in the hands of the Trustees. In July 1910 they bought seventy-five acres on Eagle Lake from Andrew Stroud Rodick. The water company bought six more lots in January 1911, including the Livingston property. By August 15, 1915, Fred Lynam was able to report to the stockholders that "of the watershed of Eagle Lake there now remains in the hands of private owners only the Brewer Ice Company property, the use of which is necessary for icing purposes, the small tea house lot owned by John Rich, a small lot near the dam and the W. M. Roberts camp lot. None of these offer at present time any problems as to the purity of Eagle Lake water. All are kept in the very best of condition."

From then on the Trustees made it a policy to acquire mountains in public water-supply watersheds and obtain power of eminent domain over the Eagle Lake and Jordan Pond watersheds. David Manski, former chief of Acadia's Division of Resource Management, explains, "Protecting water quality around Eagle Lake is how Acadia got its start, and the water company was intimately involved in this generally little-known story about the park's history."

Word of the Trustees' buying power must have spread among property owners, as Dorr, Kennedy, Stebbins, and other trustees were among the first to know whenever parcels of land went up for sale. In 1910 they found out that the western slope of Green (Cadillac) Mountain, Pemetic Mountain, and South Bubble, properties of the bankrupt Mount Desert and Eastern Shore Land Company, sold in foreclosure and were being eyed by lumber companies. Piece by piece, Dorr and his associates bought parcels and added them to the Trustees' holdings.

Believing he understood public sentiment, Charles W. Eliot reported that the land trust avoided lands that could be used either for houses or for growing food, or land within the public water distribution system. He told the Massachusetts-based Trustees of Public Reservations:

> *The operations of the trustees have already been carried far enough to make it sure that Mt. Desert Island will remain a health and pleasure resort through centuries, its wild scenery and its safe water supplies being preserved and improved. No opposition whatever has arisen to the proceedings of the trustees, and all the dwellers on the island hope that the trustees may acquire the greater part of the uninhabitable areas in the eastern half of the island and some of the finest spots in the western half.*

Yet discontent was, in fact, brewing. Logging companies were suspicious of an organization led by summer residents with the power of eminent domain. Local residents, upset about land being removed from the tax rolls and resentful that the summer people had succeeded in banning automobiles from the island, tried to revoke the Trustees' incorporation. In February 1913 Representative William Sherman of Bar Harbor (then still called Eden) introduced a bill in the state legislature to revoke the charter of the Hancock County Trustees of Public Reservations and tax-exempt status of the thousands of acres under their ownership. Dorr, hearing word of what "them fellers" were up to, went immediately to Augusta and within one evening had won the leaders of the legislature to his side. The bill was voted "ought not to pass."

While the Trustees continued to purchase and accept donations of land and money throughout this period—more than fifty separate transactions occurred—the narrow escape motivated them to involve the federal government. They needed more protection than the State of Maine could afford. They need a national monument.

The 1906 Act for the Preservation of American Antiquities ("Antiquities Act") authorized the president to set aside as national monuments lands in the public domain that possess great scientific or historic interest, or contain some great historic landmark. President Theodore Roosevelt created the first national monument, Devils Tower in Wyoming, and more than thirty followed, all in the West, including El Morro and Chaco Canyon in New Mexico, Montezuma Castle and the Petrified Forest and Grand Canyon in Arizona, and Muir Woods in California.

Dorr went to Washington to propose the idea and submitted an official proposal in the spring of 1914, which was rejected because of the discontinuous boundary around the proposed monument. To garner public support, Dorr, ornithologist Ernest Forbush, botanist Merritt Fernald, and Charles W. Eliot wrote a series of articles published in *National Geographic* magazine, as they simultaneously worked to acquire more land.

—◦—

Making the land contiguous, and clarifying all the boundaries and deeds, was an expensive task beyond the capacity of Dorr, who had already spent great sums on land purchases. He went to Charles W. Eliot for help, and Eliot, realizing the magnitude of their need, turned to John D. Rockefeller Jr.

The two men had met in 1903, when Rockefeller asked Eliot to join the board of the Rockefeller Foundation shortly after it was formed. Eliot, who was in his seventies, became a mentor and friend to the young Rockefeller.

John D. Rockefeller Jr. grew up surrounded by gardens, trees, and horses. His father, Standard Oil titan John D. Rockefeller, loved working outside and indeed spent more time on landscaping than home improvements, designing gardens, clearing scenic vistas, building racetracks for his horses, and creating swimming ponds, bike paths, and ice-skating rinks at his estates in Forest Hills and Pocantico. He employed his son, paying him to chop wood, plant trees, and manage paths. Eliot wrote that the modifications "brought the wild landscape into high culture."

John D. Jr. learned that the investment in land, and its development for recreation, was much preferred to ostentatious displays of wealth. As a youth, he overcame debilitating stress and anxiety by chopping wood, breaking stones, burning brush, and raking leaves. In nature, he could shed the restrictions of being a Rockefeller and forget, if briefly, about the tarnished reputation and responsibility of his name.

He traveled extensively in the parks of the American West, and in 1908 he, his wife Abby, and six children began spending summers on Mount Desert Island. Confident, square-jawed, strong-browed, Rockefeller retired from Standard Oil and US Steel in 1910 and purchased a 150-acre retreat around Barr Hill in Seal Harbor. He bought more land and began building carriage roads on his property as he shifted his focus full-time to philanthropy. He said the wilderness of Acadia refreshed his overburdened mind.

Like Eliot, Rockefeller wanted others to have the same opportunity; his own father had kept their family estate lands open to the public. The wealthy and powerful, however selfish their interest in exclusivity and "rustic simplicity," nevertheless made it possible for everyone to access the same landscapes.

Turning his design-minded attention to the Trustees' holdings, Rockefeller saw that most of the protected area consisted of mountaintops with very few connections. If his carriage road network was going to expand, he would need more space. He helped the Trustees fill in the gaps and conduct the necessary surveys. In return, he would be allowed to build carriage roads on public lands.

In less than two years, most of Jordan Pond and Sargent and Pemetic Mountains were protected, as were the eastern Eagle Lake shoreline and Green (Cadillac), Dry (Dorr), and Newport (Champlain) Mountains.

Dorr went back to Washington and made his offer:

On behalf of the Hancock County Trustees of Public Reservations, State of Maine, I have the honor to offer in free gift to the United States a unique and noble tract of land upon our eastern seacoast, for the establishment of a national monument. The tract offered is rich in historic association, in scientific interest, and in landscape beauty. And it contains within itself the only heights that immediately front the open sea with mountainous character upon our eastern coast.

It contains also, owing to past glacial action and its own variously resistant rocky structure, an extraordinary variety of topographic feature which unites with the climate caused by the surrounding sea to fit it beyond any other single locality in the East for the shelter, growth, and permanent preservation of a wide range of life, both plant and animal.

It forms a striking and instructive geologic record. And it constitutes the dominant and characteristic portion of the first land. Mount Desert Island, to be visited, described, and named by Champlain

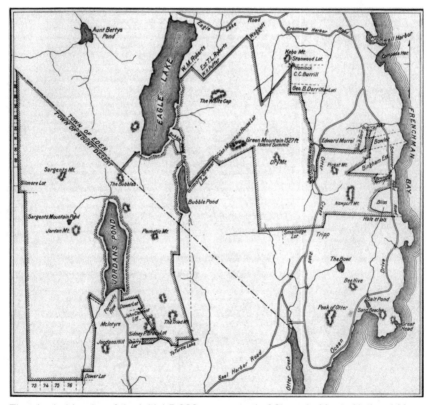

The shaded border of the initial 5,000-acre parcel of Sieur de Monts National Monument. ACADIA NATIONAL PARK

when sailing under De Monts's orders in exploration of the New England coast.

On July 8, 1916, President Woodrow Wilson proclaimed five thousand acres of Mount Desert Island as Sieur de Monts National Monument. In his statement, he cited Champlain's "exploration and discovery of great historic interest" and noted that "the topographic configuration, the geology, the fauna and the flora of the island, largely embraced within the limits of the Monument, also, are of great scientific interest."

It was the first national monument in the East, the first national reservation on the seacoast, and the first park created entirely from land donated by individuals.

Edward Rand and the surviving members of the Champlain Society must have felt some pride in hearing the news, knowing that their

The Beehive as viewed from Great Head, with Sand Beach in between. C. SCHMITT

youthful summers spent cataloging the island's natural riches were well spent. Samuel Eliot knew his brother, had he been alive, would have been relieved that at least some of his beloved Mount Desert was permanently protected. And, perhaps, father Charles W. Eliot took some small amount of solace in a vision fulfilled.

The new national monument did not include Eliza Homans's Bowl and Beehive tract, as it was not contiguous with the Eagle Lake–Green (Cadillac) Mountain parcel. Large swaths of private property lay between the new monument and the Bowl and Beehive, which were still protected, however, as Hancock County Trustees of Public Reservations lands.

Eliza Homans did not live to see the creation of Acadia. She died in 1914 of "heart trouble" at her Acadia home. But if she knew what she had started, she would feel affirmed and confirmed. Her life contributed to the benefit of the larger society—a goal that once was part of the republican ideal that her generous and compassionate nature tried to foster.

Addition

Acadia National Park Grows to Include Schoodic Point and Isle au Haut

It is our one eastern national park and gives for the first time to the crowded eastern portion of the country the opportunity to share directly and immediately in the benefits of our national park system.
—Theodore Roosevelt, letter to Congress regarding the proposal for Lafayette National Park

South and east of Mount Desert Island, a high island of spruce and rock lies between Penobscot Bay and the open Atlantic. Sea ducks paddle the waves, riding the surf almost to where it lashes cobble beaches and volcanic cliffs. The island's few coves and inlets offered harbor to the Wabanaki, and later in the eighteenth century, the island's seaworthiness appealed to the descendants of European settlers, who called it by Champlain's name, Isle au Haut.

"Too charming to be neglected by the races of the uncanny," as Arlo Bates described it, Isle au Haut remained a small fishing community until 1879, when landscape architect Ernest Bowditch stopped on the way home from working some jobs on Mount Desert. The island presented a wild and uncrowded contrast to Bar Harbor. While nowhere near as popular as Mount Desert Island, Isle au Haut did attract some Wordsworth-quoting traveler-writers, such as Moses Sweetser:

Isle-au-Haut lies well out in the sea, to the eastward of Vinalhaven, twenty-five miles from Rockland, and is destined to become one of the

foremost summer-resorts of Maine, several thousand acres of it hav-
ing been purchased and laid out by Boston, New York, and Chicago
gentlemen. The little Congregational Church near by has for a vane a
strange and extraordinary fish. There are no horses on Isle-au-Haut,
and many of the islanders have never seen this noblest friend of man-
kind. A few cattle serve for the meagre farming operations. The grand
feature of this insular land of dreams is its mountains, rising from
the shores to the height of six hundred feet, clad with a vast number
of berrybushes and strawberry-vines, and visible for many leagues
over the sea and bay, almost always wrapped in a rich purple haze,
approaching "the light that never was, on land or sea."

The local residents welcomed a visitor of such renown as Bowditch, who descended from legendary mariner and *American Practical Naviga-tor* author Nathaniel Bowditch, hero to those who made a living on the water.

Ernest Bowditch vacationed on the island a few years after his first visit, and began to identify tracts of land for purchase and to plan his Point Lookout Improvement Company. "Aristocratic yet rustic," the Point Lookout resort included summer homes, a dock, and a clubhouse. Bowditch acquired more lands on the southern and interior portion of

Postcard view of the Point Lookout Club House, Isle au Haut. DAVID HOFFMAN POSTCARD COLLECTION, FOGLER LIBRARY

the island and encouraged recreation through trails and management by an employed forester. While the majority of the island remained home to year-round fishermen and others whose livelihoods depended on the sea, Point Lookout demonstrated the vacation value of Isle au Haut, and created a community of seasonal residents who also loved the island and cared about its future.

━ ⸱

Across the water of Jericho and Blue Hill Bays, George Dorr and the Hancock County Trustees of Public Reservations strategized how to increase the area of conserved land on Mount Desert Island immediately after the creation of Sieur de Monts National Monument in 1916. As Dorr himself explained at the dedication ceremony for the monument, "What we have now achieved is a beginning only and our needs are many. We have entered on an important work . . . Let us not stop short of its fulfillment in essential points. We need more land, much more . . ."

At a national level, Congress readied to increase and organize the nation's public lands. Within two months of President Wilson's designation of the Sieur de Monts monument, Congress passed the Organic Act creating the National Park Service with its charge "to conserve the scenery and the natural and historic objects and the wild life therein and to provide for the enjoyment of the same in such manner and by such means as will leave them unimpaired for the enjoyment of future generations." The National Park Service took on the responsibility for national monuments (designated by the president), reservations, and some fourteen national parks (designated by Congress), all in the West (including Yellowstone, Sequoia, and Mount Rainier).

Acadia's proponents wanted park status, and they found an ally in Secretary of the Interior Franklin Lane, who traveled to Mount Desert in August 1917 at Dorr's invitation and stayed at Old Farm, Dorr's family home. During the day Dorr and Henry Lane Eno, a summer resident and renowned ornithologist, showed Lane the lands belonging in the monument and prospects for additional public lands.

In the flawless visit, the beauties and possibilities of Acadia soothed Lane's "tired politics-soaked soul." To Lane, man's mastering of wilderness was the true display: the spring house at Sieur de Monts, the trails, the "opened woods." Lane could see that, with time and money, the park could be a kind of "demonstration school" to show Americans how much they could add to the beauty of nature.

Dorr worked on acquiring another five thousand acres of land to add to the national reservation. Passionate, certainly; driven and dedicated, definitely; Dorr's single-minded obsession with Acadia could also cause him to be impulsive, risky, even preposterous. He kept so much knowledge in his head, he frustrated Charles William Eliot and others who wanted organization and documentation. But Dorr had time, money, and vision. He knew politics, and how to talk to politicians.

Lane pledged his support for national park status, citing Mount Desert Island's historic status due to Champlain's visit in 1604; the distinctive combination of mountain and sea; diverse, luxuriant, and "primeval" forests, shrubs, wildflowers, rocks, and wildlife; and proximity to easterners in need of recreation. Creating parks in the East, Lane believed, would

George Dorr and Interior Secretary Franklin Lane on Green (Cadillac) Mountain, 1917. ACADIA NATIONAL PARK

"preserve the fragrant restfulness of wilderness life close to the great centers of industry and commerce."

Dorr and Lane found a receptive Congress. When the national monument was established, Dorr received $150 in funds from the Interior Department (a large amount at the time), which he spent on ranger service for wildlife and bird protection. He had to wait until the 1917 fiscal year to ask for more funding.

Members of the federal appropriations committee, in reviewing his request, suggested the name Sieur de Monts be changed to something more familiar and relevant. The ensuing discussion brought up the need to change not only the name, but the official status from monument to park.

In May 1918, George Dorr and Maine Republican representative John Peters found themselves before the House of Representatives subcommittee on public lands with a proposal for "Mount Desert National Park."

In hearing about the origin of the proposed name, which referenced Champlain's "deserted mountains," Peters's fellow representatives became anxious. Aren't parks supposed to have trees?

"Are the proposed park lands covered with timber, in an amount sufficient to make it an attractive place for a park?" they asked.

"Oh yes, more than that," answered Dorr.

"It is the most beautiful and most useful place for a public park that there is anywhere in the East," said Peters, of Ellsworth, Maine.

The subcommittee also viewed migratory waterfowl and opportunities for fishing as important components of a "park." Their concern about protection of game reflected the era's larger conservation consciousness. They were assured that ducks, geese, and fish abounded.

Dorr then presented a full and complete description of the property: its range of deeply divided mountains carved by the ice sheet, sheltered bays and waterways, deep valleys, forests, wildflowers.

"It is actually a national park," said Peters. "It is treated as such, used as such, and in order to get the benefit of a national park, it is desired to have it technically and legally a national park."

Congress agreed and created Lafayette National Park in February 1919, declaring, "The tracts of land, easements, and other real estate heretofore known as the Sieur de Monts National Monument . . . is hereby declared to be a national park and dedicated as a public park for the benefit and enjoyment of the people under the name of the Lafayette National Park."

Dorr chose the name Lafayette to honor the historical French presence in Acadia, and to appeal to a Congress preoccupied with war in Europe. Squadrons of American pilots, fighting alongside their French allies, took the name Lafayette after the man who supported George Washington in the Revolutionary War.

In his analysis of the new park, wilderness advocate Robert Sterling Yard observed, "The one eastern representative of the National Park Service upholds to the full, under the different conditions of landscape and flora, the best standards set by the ruggeder west. Let Lafayette, therefore, serve as the standard bearer for the other eastern national parks which it is the people's business to procure."

Park status secure, Dorr's efforts to expand and complete the park did not stop, and John D. Rockefeller Jr. got more and more involved. Rockefeller had been collaborating with Dorr, now superintendent of the national park, and the Hancock County Trustees of Public Reservations on property management and acquisition. In September 1919, Rockefeller transferred his first outright gift of land to the park: one hundred acres on Beech Hill and another hundred acres on the cliffed shore of Dennings Pond (Echo Lake).

Supporters credited the Trustees and Rockefeller with protecting Mount Desert from unsightly advertising, gas stations, resorts, and the constant danger of forest fires. High on adrenaline from his successes, Dorr pressed on, negotiating transactions between Rockefeller and the National Park Service in relative quiet . . . until Rockefeller's expanding network of carriage roads approached the Amphitheater.

A great, deep glacial valley on the southern flank of Sargent/Penobscot Mountains, filled with forest and drained by crystal-clear Little Harbor Brook, the Amphitheater still felt wild in 1919. Some of the summer residents protested, fearing the loss of "unbroken forest" and wilderness character of the valley, one of the most magical and remote areas on the eastern side of Mount Desert Island.

Ever sensitive to public perception, Rockefeller put the Amphitheater trail on pause as he developed other carriage and auto roads. Rockefeller did whatever it took to move the work forward on other parts of Mount Desert. He provided the funds (and in some cases acquired the land), his engineers Paul Simpson and Walters Hill engineered the work, and his contractors built the roads. Carriage roads cut through rock slides and curved around hillsides, brushed waterfalls, and towered over streams and footpaths. Magnificent stone archways bridged the larger valleys.

Since the creation of the national monument in 1916, other gifts of land continued to be made: hills, brooks, and valleys; part of Bar Island. All of the mountaintops except Brown (Norumbega) were protected, as were Jordan Pond and Eagle Lake, the southern half of Echo Lake, and Long Pond. But the park had no comprehensive management strategy, no master plan.

Concerned over carriage road expansion to the Amphitheater and beyond, the Bar Harbor Village Improvement Association decided to procure a study of the island in the fall of 1926 from Charles William Eliot II, grandson of Harvard president Charles W. Eliot, son of Samuel Eliot, and nephew of the deceased Charles Eliot. His birth less than two years after the death of his uncle preordained Eliot II to be a landscape architect. He, too, apprenticed in the legendary Olmsted firm and became landscape and park planner for a major city. Despite his new position with the National Capital Park and Planning Commission in Washington, DC, he took the Acadia job and in 1928 completed the study titled "The Future of Mount Desert Island."

Eliot designated ten areas as "wilderness areas," including the Amphitheater and the Bowl. Roads should not be allowed in these areas, only footpaths, for "wood-wise" visitors who could "appreciate without destroying." Recreational infrastructure should concentrate around centers like the Jordan Pond House, he wrote.

The report had limited distribution, reaction, and impact, especially with so much land and money under the control of Dorr and Rockefeller. The Hancock County Trustees of Public Reservations continued to act as a holding company, accepting gifts of land and working with the Department of the Interior through a lengthy process to add to park lands.

In September 1922 George Dorr went to dinner at the Jordan Pond House, where he ran into Louise Leeds, the widow of Schoodic Point's John G. Moore, and had a conversation that would result in the park expanding beyond Mount Desert Island.

Moore grew up in nearby Steuben, but he left and made his fortune on telegraph lines and railroads. In 1889 he and a group of wealthy New Yorkers and Philadelphians created the Gouldsboro Land Improvement Company and founded the Grindstone Neck summer colony at Winter Harbor, away from the commercializing tourist world of Bar Harbor.

Moore built a large "cottage" and began buying property on the Schoodic Peninsula. He built a new carriage road along the shore from Lower Harbor to the summit of Schoodic Head Mountain. In 1899 he bought a thousand-acre lot of forested land that included the watershed of Birch Harbor Mountain, the old sawmill at Mill Creek, and Wonsqueak Bay. A few months later, he died of a heart attack, leaving the property in the hands of Louise. She and her daughters held on to the land, keeping it intact and unsold. But taxes were becoming a strain on family finances.

At their impromptu Jordan Pond House meeting, Louise Leeds asked Dorr if he was interested in the property at Schoodic Point. He said yes.

Five years later, Faith and Ruth Moore donated their father's property at Schoodic Point to the National Park Service. They had one condition of sale, however: As people of English descent, and then living in England, they wanted the park's name changed from "Lafayette" to something less French and more broad and relevant.

Dorr needed a new act of Congress to allow the park to acquire property beyond Mount Desert Island, so he was able to incorporate the name change into the same legislation. He chose *Acadia* because of its historical associations and descriptive character.

On January 19, 1929, Acadia National Park was officially given its name. When Louise Leeds and her daughters deeded the Schoodic District to the federal government, they required that the land be kept "forever as a free public park or for other public purposes and for such

Southeasterly view of Schoodic Point. ACADIA NATIONAL PARK

other uses as are incidental to the same, including the promotion of biological and other scientific research."

After the addition of Schoodic Point, the Depression and then the New Deal changed the prospects of owning land. Many property owners felt financial pressure to sell land they could no longer afford, while New Deal funds from the Resettlement Administration allowed Dorr to acquire more land. Most of the newly acquired properties were on the western side of the island: Pretty Marsh, lands between Hodgdon Pond and Long Pond, Western Mountain, and a large tract extending from the southeast shore of Seal Cove Pond, through Lurvey and Marshall Brook watersheds, Big Heath, and a stretch of coastline from Seawall Pond to Bass Harbor Head. On Schoodic Peninsula, the park acquired additional small parcels from the Winter Harbor Improvement Company.

The Hancock County Trustees of Public Reservations remained an active partner in acquiring land. In 1936 Samuel Eliot wrote:

All who are interested in one of the most beautiful regions in North America will recognize that it is exceedingly desirable that certain areas still held in private ownership should be included either in the Park or in the lands held by the Trustees. As illustrations of properties that are needed to round out the Park or to protect the views from the hilltops there may be mentioned the ridge and top of Brown [Norumbega] Mountain, a strip of land on the northern ridge of Newport [Champlain] which cuts through and severs park holdings, and the Porcupine Islands in Frenchman's Bay. While all the towns on the island have now established public landings there is still need of more access to the shores and for the preservation for public enjoyment of some of the fine headlands and beaches.

By 1940 the land area of the park had doubled to more than ten thousand acres.

The New Deal began to heal the wounds caused by the Great Depression, but not until the Second World War did Americans again feel pride, which contributed to an attitude of sacrifice and compassion. People searched for ways to serve their country at war and at home, among them three of Ernest Bowditch's children: Richard, Sarah, and Elizabeth. They had inherited their father's land on Isle au Haut after his death in 1918, but like the Moore family, were having trouble keeping up with management of the property. They knew life was changing, and they knew the park had inquired about the island. Within weeks of the attack at Pearl Harbor, on February 4, 1942, Richard Bowditch called the Department of the Interior to see if they were interested in the properties; the government accepted in January 1944.

The Bowditch family donated the park land without consulting the rest of the Isle au Haut community, who were accustomed to living in a remote location, with autonomy and unrestricted access to natural resources. Surprised and angry, they resisted their new "neighbor." Residents, especially those whose families had lived on Isle au Haut for generations, suddenly faced an uncertain future in which their favorite and most meaningful places lay within park boundaries.

While little changed at first, Isle au Haut's experience with the National Park Service would eventually become much more conflicted, as perceptions of Acadia differed among residents, summer people, and park visitors.

Seasonal residents, most active in creating and expanding the park, based their perceptions on a summertime residency. Visitors "from away" who did not live on Mount Desert, Isle au Haut, or Schoodic year-round, they did not make their living directly from the land or water. Despite their dependence on the local community to enable and enhance their amusement, the summer people also had insulated themselves from the locals, devising their own unique leisure activities like golf, swimming, and yachting, and forming expensive clubs that effectively excluded locals from membership. They saw themselves apart from the people of Acadia, yet claimed a unique understanding of the place of Acadia.

During the hearings to change Acadia's status from monument to park, the congressional appropriations committee asked if any large cities were in close proximity to the proposed park.

Dorr replied, "Bangor is the nearest. But this park would be used principally by people from beyond the state, not by Maine people. I went there myself from Boston as a boy. My father bought some land there then, on part of which we built a summer home and part of which has now been donated to the Government. The friends I have made there have come from the whole country to the eastward of the Rockies, from New Orleans, from St. Louis, from Cincinnati and Chicago, and largely from the South. We used to have a number of Richmond people and Confederate service officers and their families there regularly at one time, and many people come there always from Washington and Baltimore, from Philadelphia and New York. It is a place of national resort, not in any sense a local area."

"How many people live near the proposed park?" members of the committee asked.

Congressman Peters responded, "I live nearby there and I know the natives who live around there. I don't suppose that one man out of 100 who lives there knows of the beauty of this place; but if it is developed as a national park the local people will take more interest in it."

Botanical specimens preserved in museums testify that people from across the state of Maine came to Acadia throughout the late nineteenth and early twentieth centuries. Yet many park advocates did not think the "local" year-round residents valued Acadia. Dorr and Peters exhibited this assumption in their comments at the congressional hearing. Early guidebook authors, in preparing tourists for the people they would meet in Acadia, also judged the locals.

Clara Barnes Martin, appalled at the living conditions of some local families (and lack of agriculture), suggested in the first few editions of her guide that the people of Mount Desert would benefit from "a better acquaintance with the rest of the world."

In his 1875 *Nooks and Corners of the New England Coast*, Samuel Adams Drake wrote of Mount Desert, "None could be more astonished at their own prosperity than these islanders, who, being, as a whole and in a marked degree, incapable of appreciating the grandeur of the scenes with which they have from infancy been familiar, look with scarce concealed disdain upon the admiration they inspire in others."

Visitors and summer folk believed that their presence, and tourism in general, had improved life for year-round residents.

As Charles W. Eliot described, the summer people's desire for pretty roads employed men, horses, and vehicles. Their need of fresh, local milk, eggs, chickens, vegetables, clams, scallops, lobsters, and fish created a "legitimate" source of profit for numerous island residents. Local men could tend the sailboats, manage the waterfront, and deliver coal, wood, and ice; local women had plenty of laundry to do. Young people could find jobs at hotels and boardinghouses.

This "right" development of Acadia would preserve a varied landscape of woods, pastures, cultivated fields, gardens, barns, and houses—scenery "on the whole more interesting than the monotonous sweep of an unbroken forest," Eliot wrote in 1904. A park-centric management approach could include existing industries, as long as "the squalor of a city, with all its inevitable bustle, dirt, and ugliness" was forever excluded from the island. "It is to escape the sights and sounds of the city that intelligent people come in summer to such a place as this rough and beautiful island; and the shortseason populations do not wish to be reminded in summer of the scenes and noises amid which the greater part of their lives is inevitably passed." One person's year-round reality was another person's seasonal escape.

Charles William Eliot II echoed this sentiment, writing that a permanent resident of Mount Desert Island depended on the summer business for income, and should take action to keep and enhance tourism: "The beauty of the Island and the Park, and the resort character of the community, are his most important assets. He not only lives with the problems involved more continuously than do the members of any other group, but also has the voting power to materially affect the manner of their solution."

Communication among visitors, seasonal residents, and the year-rounders shifted when the automobile brought the different populations in closer proximity and conflict, and more people came to tour the first national park east of the Mississippi River. But the differences among the populations persisted.

Those who only visited the island in summer wanted Acadia to remain exactly as it was every summer, preserved in time as it was in their memories, a place away from their workaday lives. Ignorant of the hardships of winter in such a remote and rugged landscape, unfamiliar with the sometimes desperate employment situations of an economically depressed state like Maine, the summer people and the park that served them seemed to think their attachment to Acadia, their sense of place, superseded any connections year-round residents may have had to the landscape.

The local newspapers favored the wealthy summer people and echoed the idea that the local residents never went into Acadia. A *Bar Harbor Record* editorial of March 31, 1920, implored residents to enjoy the snowy trail system through the park. In asking residents to use the trails, the editor suggested that they would not only obtain personal pleasures, but would "acquire information of great value." According to the *Record* editor, the principal business in Bar Harbor was the "selling of the scenery and if we do not know our own product, how can we sell it?" The editor recommended that "in every home and business establishment of Mount Desert Island there should be a good map of the national park."

Acadia National Park staff, 1941. ACADIA NATIONAL PARK

The 1929 legislation that renamed the park and added the Schoodic District created a park with no permanent boundary and no authority to purchase land; it could only accept donations. Superintendent Dorr designed roads, campgrounds, and a visitor center, but he lacked a management plan for the park in its entirety. And local communities lacked a voice in park decisions, which is what happened at Otter Creek when John D. Rockefeller Jr. acquired the waterfront with goals to remake the inner cove as a swimming pond enclosed in a scenic causeway. He closed off access to the waterfront and its fish houses, severing the resident community from its traditional way of life. The National Park Service also changed their activity on Isle au Haut, tearing down fish houses and enforcing bans on hunting and gathering firewood.

The patchwork of donated land parcels scattered across the region complicated management, protection, and visitor orientation, and frustrated local towns with the constant threat of unexpected donations eroding their tax bases and limiting access to lands used for hunting, fishing, and other traditional uses.

When the National Park Service released a study of conservation objectives that suggested further consolidation and expansion, towns, residents, and private organizations formulated a coordinated response, printed as a petition in the *Bar Harbor Times* in August 1962 "that the National Park Service acquire no additional lake or ocean shore property on the Island of Mount Desert." Fearing eminent domain and further park expansion, they wanted to know the park's intentions for existing and future property. Missing the property tax revenues, they suggested a fee system for revenue. Concerned about lack of trail maintenance and overgrown scenic views, they demanded the park create opportunities for "more recreational use."

In a 1966 draft plan, the park recommended acquiring some of the same tracts cited as off limits in the petition, such as Indian Point, "the best area and one of the very few areas on the islands where seals can be observed." Acquiring inholdings, private property surrounded by park lands, would eliminate the possibility of development and allow the park's resource management staff to apply more consistent fire and pest control and tree protection. At Schoodic, the park hoped to eliminate the threat of clear-cutting for pulpwood, which was a problem in areas within sight of Schoodic Head. Other targeted areas included the south end of Seal Cove Pond, the north end of Long Pond and Round Pond, and the eastern Mount Desert shoreline from Bear Brook to Schooner Head.

Town and county officials, angry and frustrated with the new federal presence in their midst, feared losing potentially more property tax revenues if the park received more land and held more conservation easements. They pressured the park to end the speculation and uncertainty and establish a permanent boundary.

The 1960s and 1970s brought unprecedented numbers of visitors and escalating traffic problems. On Isle au Haut, more tourists began arriving unprepared for what they would encounter. Dropped off at the town landing, tourists seemed to think the whole island was their playground.

They trespassed on private property, often got lost, and crowded the town. In response, summer residents (about three hundred people) and year-rounders (fewer than one hundred) began talking about shared concerns and working together to confront the park.

The great difficulty of setting a permanent boundary prolonged planning efforts into the 1980s, as the National Park Service, the towns, the Hancock County Planning Commission, and numerous conservation groups attempted resolution through what all sides described as "arduous negotiations." Agreements were drafted but never signed. With more land donated, transferred, or swapped, the park included more than forty thousand acres. Opposition greeted every map and plan that proposed further growth.

In 1982, Isle au Haut discussions led to legislation that would consolidate park property on the southern half of the island, build a campground at Duck Harbor, protect mountain summits, prohibit park expansion, and limit and control visitors. Isle au Haut's year-round villages remained separate and distinct from the park, with limited interaction between the two populations by design.

On Mount Desert Island the situation remained heated, with houses being constructed on Schooner Head and national environmental organizations like the Sierra Club advocating for greater land protections while the towns looked after their own interests—and property tax income. The office of Maine senator George Mitchell got involved.

In 1986, with intervention by Maine's senators and representatives, Congress enacted legislation to draw a line around the rest of the park and set down in law how and where the park could expand. An advisory board acknowledged that more people had a say in what Acadia should be.

The 1986 Acadia Boundary Legislation (Public Law 99-420), the result of more than twenty years of research and work, balanced areas that needed preservation with the concerns and views of local towns, landowners, and government representatives. In the end, the law created a boundary within which the National Park Service could own property on Mount Desert Island and Schoodic and a few outer islands like the Porcupines.

The southern shoreline of Isle au Haut. C. SCHMITT

Much thought and deliberation went into the final boundary line, which encompassed more than one hundred privately owned parcels. The legislation included these lots because they protected significant resources, were along the edges of the boundary, or were "holes" completely or mostly surrounded by park lands. In the legislation Congress enabled the park to acquire parcels from willing sellers or donors to "complete" or fill in the boundary.

Establishment of a permanent park boundary in 1986 eased some tensions over the federal government's future actions regarding land in Acadia. But the threats to Acadia did not end, and more and more of them were coming from beyond Acadia's borders.

Archipelago

Acadia's Place in the Larger Gulf of Maine Ecosystem

The sea, especially, kept Eden close to what was going on, as long as Eden kept close to the sea.
—RICHARD HALE, *THE STORY OF BAR HARBOR*

THE PLACE KNOWN AS ACADIA IS MORE WATER THAN LAND.

The Gulf of Maine, a semi-enclosed sea of the Atlantic Ocean, surrounds the peninsulas and encircles the islands of Acadia. The ocean brings fog, wind, salt, and waves. The ocean brings distance: Fifteen miles of water separate Isle au Haut from Mount Desert; Schoodic is five miles across Frenchman Bay. The ocean also unites, connecting hundreds of scattered islands into an archipelago greater than the sum of its parts.

The Wabanaki knew this, for they came to Acadia for its marine resources, like clams, fish, and sweetgrass, and lived near the coast year-round.

The navigators knew this, for the island offered relief after days in a monotonous sea.

The settlers knew this, for they built their homes along the shore and made a living from what they could pull from the deep or ship across the surface.

The visitors knew this. Although some people forgot about the sea, how it connected them to other places and to each other, others kept the sea close, sailing between the islands all summer long.

—⁓—

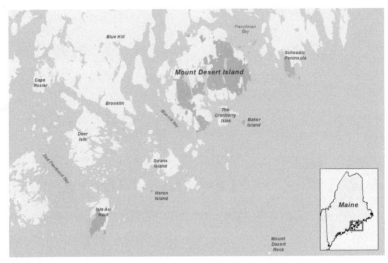

The Acadia Archipelago. Acadia National Park shown by shaded areas.
ACADIA NATIONAL PARK

The seasons of Acadia are more winter than summer. The blooms of the Azalea Garden, the fruits of summer, the blazing color of autumn—none would be possible without the cold and dark of winter. A period of snow and ice kept the jack pine, fir, and spruce that gave Acadia its boreal character, and kept the streams cool enough for brook trout. Whales and porpoises fed in the cold ocean waters that each summer greened with microscopic algae and crustaceans around Mount Desert Rock. Seals came down from the north to raise their young and haul out on ledges and islands. The pale blue flowers of marsh felwort, the southernmost population in New England, bloomed each September on the bold, rocky shoreline of Schoodic Point.

And the birds, so many birds. Petrels, cormorants, herons, terns, harlequin and eider ducks, loons, guillemots, gannets, jaegers, kittiwakes, and other seabirds inhabited the outer islands and rocks—so many birds it was easy to forget that seabirds nested on only 10 percent of Maine's islands, the only place in the country where they bred in significant numbers, or that many species had rebounded from near extinction. Schoodic Island was home to the largest single gull colony in the region. Herring gulls were so abundant in the 1930s, park naturalists considered the

The cover of the first issue of *Nature Notes*, written largely by Acadia National Park naturalist Arthur Stupka. ACADIA NATIONAL PARK

species a symbol of Acadia National Park and put a gull on the cover of *Nature Notes* and other park publications.

With no regard for boundaries or property ownership, the seasonal migrations moved through Acadia like waves.

Snowy owls; ivory, ring-billed, glaucous, and Iceland gulls; razorbills; and murres visited in winter, replacing thousands of footsteps with wing beats. In spring came the multicolored warblers from the tropics, chirping and singing and flitting through the trees at Bass Harbor. Eagles, ospreys, and peregrine falcons arrived early to establish or reclaim their treetop and cliffside aeries. Come fall, thousands of sharp-shinned hawks, kestrels, and other raptors from Maine and Canada rode the strong winds over Cadillac Mountain and along the eastern coastline as they migrated to warmer areas for the winter.

Why so many birds? The sea, remember the sea. Acadia's islands, beaches, and salt marshes lie in the path of the Atlantic Flyway, a great migration corridor for millions of birds, butterflies, bats, and dragonflies, winged creatures that need places to land, eat, sleep, and stay throughout their journey.

The birds especially were not doing well at the turn of the nineteenth century, when National Audubon Society founder Thomas Gilbert Pearson began working with the US government and private landowners to establish a chain of bird sanctuaries extending from Maine to Florida and west to the Pacific coast. Throughout their reconnaissance work, Pearson said, they found no area that could equal Acadia's importance to wildlife. Locally, some Bar Harbor "women's clubs" wanted to make all of Mount Desert a bird sanctuary.

The US Biological Survey, too, saw the area's potential as a much-needed wildlife sanctuary on the crowded East Coast. They supported George Dorr, Charles William Eliot, and John D. Rockefeller Jr. in their efforts to create a national park, and suggested that the fastest way to government acceptance of the property was to offer it as a national monument.

Bird-watchers knew that protecting habitat at home would help the birds throughout their life journeys, but in the mid-1900s they did not know the details of those journeys. What signaled them to leave? What routes did they take? How long did they stay?

Each spring and fall, the birds moved over and through the islands of Acadia. Shorebirds swarmed the mudflats and beaches. Seabirds found their islands. Hawks and eagles soared above the hills. Warblers and other songbirds took to the trees, some stopping to rest in a small valley at the head of Somes Sound on Mount Desert Island, where they ran into the nets of Barbara Patterson.

Barbara Patterson came to Mount Desert from Wayland, Massachusetts, in January 1934. Her husband, Robert Patterson, had taken a job with the Civilian Conservation Corps. A Harvard graduate trained in both building and landscape architecture, he assisted the park's landscape architect Benjamin Breeze, supervising construction of the Beech Cliff area and Perpendicular Trail. The Pattersons stayed in Acadia after the New Deal program work, moving to a house in Somesville. Robert opened his own practice and had a hand in many developments on the island, including design work with Beatrix Farrand. After the fire of 1947, he helped to rebuild the community with a distinctive modernist style that fit the Acadian environment.

During this time, Barbara raised their two children. But she must have thought about birds, watched them in the backyard, along Acadia's trails, and on family trips to the Maine North Woods. Perhaps she went to tea at the Great Head home of Effie Anthony, an avid birder who loved to share her hobby of banding birds with others. Maybe she ran into graduate student Robert MacArthur at Bass Harbor, where he studied the habits of five insect-eating warbler species, work that contributed to his theory of island biogeography developed with Edward O. Wilson.

Barbara must have read Arthur Stupka's *Nature Notes*, must have known about ornithologist James Bond's compilation of the island's birds. Both Barbara and Robert loved the outdoors and spent time backpacking and canoeing. At home they turned their yard into gardens landscaped with native plants. They would have interacted with scientists and conservationists through Robert's work.

Someone or something motivated Barbara Patterson to begin studying birds, for in 1957, her children grown, she applied for her own bird-banding license from the US Fish and Wildlife Service. The agency had just launched Operation Recovery, an effort to track birds as they migrated along the Northeast coast each fall. As monitors at southern stations recaptured banded birds, researchers hoped to track the birds in space and time.

The birds became an integral part of her day. Patterson hung Japanese mist nets, twelve feet high and forty feet across, between the trees. Every forty-five minutes she checked the nets, lowering them a little bit at a time to untangle each fluttering bird. The animals were remarkably delicate and docile as Patterson gently placed them into the six covered pockets of her apron. A member of the church sewing circle, she designed the garment herself, using breathable, dark green denim or floral fabric, with large pockets that would keep the birds calm while they waited to be processed.

Working at a sheltered, handmade wooden table near the nets, in what seemed like one quick motion, she weighed, measured, and banded each bird's leg with a numbered aluminum ring, all the while talking softly to the bird. Released, the bird gave a few chirps and flew away. During the busy fall migration, she might spend ten hours in the field.

In the winter she trapped birds closer to the house, raising and lowering feeders and trap gates with a series of pulleys leading in through the kitchen window; she hung the mist nets back in the trees come spring. Unfunded and unrecognized, Patterson paid for her own equipment: nets and scales, birdcalls, pliers, and a Kodak Startech camera. She mostly worked alone, with only occasional help from her husband, grandchildren, or a fellow birder like Reginald Allen, Bill Townsend, or Jim Bond. She enjoyed being outside, physical work, and the chance to contribute. At home, she copied measurements, dates, and bird observations onto ledgers and index cards, and prepared reports to the federal bird laboratory in Laurel, Maryland. On occasion she banded seabirds on the islands at the request of researchers.

She published a few articles and letters, but more often she provided data to other scientists: nest records to the Cornell Lab of Ornithology in New York, banding data to the Eastern Bird Banding Association, bird skins to the University of Maine. She took exquisite notes, corrected editors when they published an error, and maintained correspondence with leading scientists. She went about her work in a stoic and focused fashion. She loved the work, but no one in her family had any idea about the extent of her scientific practice.

Barbara Patterson demonstrating her bird-banding
technique, 1980. M. KANE / *BAR HARBOR TIMES*

Patterson, like other bird-banders, closely followed her birds, track-
ing individuals who returned the next season. Over twenty-three years,
she banded more than twenty-eight thousand birds. From a long-term,
detailed record from a single location, she started to piece together the
complexity of migration. While she could not know the larger forces
influencing the patterns she observed, Patterson nevertheless had an
awareness of broader environmental concerns.

Her husband, Robert, had become very concerned about development of the Allagash and St. John Rivers, where large dams were

proposed. He connected with other citizens concerned about dams, pesticides, and water quality, and in 1959 they formed the Natural Resources Council of Maine. Bob Patterson served as first president of the council. He was also on the board of the National Wildlife Federation and President Lyndon Johnson's advisory board on water pollution control. Surely he (and Barbara) would have read Rachel Carson's *Silent Spring*, must have known that chemicals like DDT could permeate even the Eden of Acadia and its birds, and in fact had already decimated one member of the fauna: the peregrine falcon.

Once sprayed into air, land, and water, the chemical pesticide DDT entered the food web, magnifying with each transfer from prey to predator. In seabirds, peregrines, eagles, and ospreys, DDT caused the birds to lay eggs with thin, weak shells that broke easily. The birds could not reproduce, and populations crashed. Not a single peregrine nested in the eastern half of the country. Barbara Patterson likely never saw a peregrine falcon at Acadia.

Philadelphia Academy of Natural Sciences biologist James Bond noted the loss of peregrine falcons in 1967:

> *Probably never more than two pairs of these falcons have inhabited Mt. Desert. I know of only two former aeries, one on the steep slope of Champlain Mountain near Bar Harbor, the other on Eagle Cliffs of St. Sauveur Mountain bordering Somes Sound. The flight of this fine falcon is exceedingly rapid . . . During the past decade the Peregrine has apparently been extirpated as a breeding bird of Mt. Desert although an occasional individual is still seen on migration, sometimes out at sea.*

Other damage to Acadia was more visible. More and more houses and summer cottages were appearing throughout the archipelago, affecting the experience of being on the water and impacting the scenery viewed from landscapes that George Dorr and others had so carefully stitched together.

One evening in the late 1960s, Peggy Rockefeller marched into a friend's cottage and said, "We've got to DO something!" The outgoing and outspoken spouse of David Rockefeller, John D. Rockefeller Jr.'s youngest son, was fed up. The Rockefellers, sailors and lifetime summer residents of Maine, had watched how development had transformed Acadia over the recent decades, and they were people with the means to do something about what they viewed as a loss of scenic character. With the help of their savvy New York lawyers, they pursued options for protecting more land in the archipelago.

"An open space program can't be planned in bits and pieces; it must have some topographical unity," wrote William H. Whyte in a 1959 bulletin by the Urban Land Institute. Whyte proposed more widespread application of the conservation easement, a legal agreement between a landowner and a conservation organization that restricts what activities can occur on a property in order to protect specific land, water, wildlife, or scenic values.

As an example of citizen-led land protection, Whyte held up The Trustees of Reservations in Massachusetts, the organization that inspired Acadia's own Hancock County Trustees. Created by the young Charles Eliot, the original Trustees acquired thousands of acres and helped establish the Metropolitan District Commission in Boston, which protected green space along Commonwealth Avenue and the Charles River in the 1880s. Like Eliot, Whyte saw the potential for individual property owners, one at a time and neighbor by neighbor, to protect large areas.

And that's exactly what Peggy Rockefeller did, working her network of friends and contacts who also loved Acadia. Similar concerns about development could be found across Maine. Robert Patterson, through his role with the Natural Resources Council of Maine, worked with the state legislature to create a new law authorizing government agencies to accept conservation easements from private property owners.

At the same time, Patterson helped Peggy Rockefeller, whose strategy involved identifying other landowners who, like her, might be willing to conserve all or part of their property. For help, she called German Emory, who was involved in island conservation in the Eggemoggin

Reach area. On their hands and knees, they poured over charts of the archipelago spread out on Rockefeller's living room rug.

Another friend, sailor and Boston businessman Tom Cabot, kept the library on his yawl *Avelinda* stuffed with information about the islands and their owners. Others involved included Portland attorney Harold "Ed" Woodsum and Acadia superintendent John Good and chief ranger Bob Binnewies. In 1970, they formed the nonprofit Maine Coast Heritage Trust to promote and negotiate conservation easements to be granted to Acadia National Park.

Immediately the trust, with Peggy Rockefeller at the helm of the board of directors, promoted conservation easements on islands. Elmer Beal, who came from a fishing family in Southwest Harbor, served as the first executive director. Ben Emory, fresh out of the US Navy and on summer break from his MBA program, helped Beal and the board of directors sell the idea to landowners, one at a time, by letter and telephone and kitchen-table conversation.

The first conservation easement given to Acadia National Park, on Little Spoon Island off Isle au Haut, made Acadia the first agency in Maine to accept such a donation.

Land protection was contagious, spreading among those lucky enough to own beautiful places who wanted to leave a legacy for their own families and future generations. However, many people involved were not wealthy landowners, but people inspired by the fledgling environmental movement. And many, many more benefited from preservation of the island scenery and ecology.

The National Park Service, at the time involved in the master planning that would be so contentious until the 1986 boundary legislation, looked outward to the sea, writing in one planning doument, "Acadia National Park is a coastal national park. Its paramount values are those associated with the sea—its seascape scenery, its marine plants and animals, and its marine history. Acadia is basically an archipelago park, for between and near its major segments be some 250 smaller islands and islets. These offshore islands are an inseparable part of the Acadia scene."

One of Maine Coast Heritage Trust's letters reached Charles Lakin on Burnt Island, who was in the process of trying to plan his estate and figure out a way to preserve Burnt, Mouse, and Wheat Islands, clustered at the north end of Isle au Haut. The idea of continuing ownership but preserving in perpetuity the scenic and natural resources of the islands, which had been in his family's ownership since the late 1800s, appealed to Lakin. He, too, donated a conservation easement to Acadia National Park.

More donated easements followed: Buckle and Duck Islands (from Peggy Rockefeller), Butter Island, Big Babson Island, Fernald Point in Southwest Harbor. Most of these early easements intended to preserve "natural and scenic values," with the understanding that preservation of the natural resources went along with conserving scenery.

What was scenic?

According to one report, people agreed that "scenic" land had water, distant views (with "diverse and well-maintained" vegetation in the foreground), and a "folded" landscape of mountains and islands. Echoing the old nineteenth-century language of the sublime and picturesque, people generally considered scenic land to be undeveloped land, unless the development consisted of "traditional" Maine coastal scenes like cedar-clad Cape-style cottages, docks and fish shacks adorned with lobster buoys, farm fields or stone walls. Scenic property had a sense of mystery, of wanting to be drawn further into the scene. Groups of islands presented "physiographic unity." The Acadian archipelago's relatively undeveloped character made it unusual in the United States; it continued to be viewed as Eden, a "Twilight in the Wilderness."

But a park couldn't be managed on appearances alone. Plants hadn't been mapped or inventoried since the work of Barrington Moore and Edgar Wherry in the 1920s. Deer, "infrequently reported" in 1932 according to park naturalist Arthur Stupka, had increased in numbers after the 1947 fire. What were the populations of skunk, red fox, and river otter (thought to be extinct from Mount Desert in 1932)? What did it mean that coyotes had recently arrived on Mount Desert Island? Would peregrines ever come back?

In March 1980 Barbara Patterson wrote to Richard Ferren, regional coordinator of the *Atlantic Flyway Review,*

> *My banding permit expires at the end of August and, with much soul searching (and a few tears), I've asked not to have it renewed. It's becoming too much of a physical chore with no young and energetic helpers. I am going to try to get in 2 weeks of netting this summer— mid August to the end. If the results are good I'll send them in the next year. I feel particularly badly because <u>more</u> banders are needed down east, not fewer.*

Through her work documenting other bird populations, in parallel with her husband's activism, Barbara Patterson participated in the environmental awakening of the 1960s and 1970s. Federal laws like the National Environmental Policy Act and advances in scientific understanding led to an increasing awareness that conserving one's own backyard was not enough. This awareness found its way into the 1986 boundary legislation for Acadia National Park, which recognized that protection of the larger Acadian archipelago landscape was essential for not only scenic purposes, but for ecological reasons as well.

———

Judy Hazen Connery had just started her position as a biological technician in the new division of resource management. With a bachelor's degree in natural resource management from Cornell, she had been working as a park ranger, supervising the visitor centers during the summer and doing clerical work in the winter. In her new role, she was selected to participate in the National Park Service's new professional natural resource management training program, spending weeks at a time at universities around the country.

Back in Bar Harbor, she and the other two resource management staff squeezed their desks into a corner of the ranger office. They made sure the long-term vision (and funding) for the general management plan of 1992 included resource stewardship, establishing as the primary management focus "protecting and perpetuating the natural resource base upon which the park was established."

To succeed, they needed to know more about the natural resources themselves—basic information about the nature of Acadia. They updated vegetation maps and plant lists, and found a large percentage of invasive plants, many of which were established as settlers transformed forest and meadow into farms, landscaped estates, and gardens. They surveyed soils and wetlands, sampled water quality in lakes and streams, and funded studies of the intertidal zone. And they learned of problems too. A garbage landfill was leaking into Bass Harbor marsh, and Abraham Somes's old dams prevented alewives and other sea-run fish from moving upstream.

Perhaps their most unfortunate discovery had to do with air quality. The park had joined a national air-quality monitoring program and installed state-of-the-art sampling equipment. The program's scientists selected Acadia as a control site, a remote location that would serve as a measure of "clean" air compared to parks in more urban areas. Within the first year, however, sampling data showed that Acadia actually had *higher* levels of ozone and other pollutants. How could this be? Wasn't a national park supposed to be pristine?

Located at the eastern edge of the continent, Acadia sat downwind of coal-fired power plants and major cities. The coastal position created salty winds and fog that harbored haze and pollutants; the spruce, fir, and pine so characteristic of Acadia were especially good scavengers, their sticky, needled tips combing chemical particles from the air. Some of the highest ozone levels in North America were found at Acadia, and the highest ozone concentration ever recorded in Maine was measured at Isle au Haut on June 15, 1988. The same coal plants that produced ozone and smog also produced toxic mercury, which was carried in the clouds and deposited on Acadia with rain, snow, and dust. Smog and ozone marred the view from Acadia's summits, restricting opportunities for visitors to enjoy the park's spectacular vistas while raising awareness of the larger problem.

All of these issues, most originating outside of Acadia's borders, made it clear that closing the garden gate would not keep out the world. And so Acadia also became a stage for demonstrating solutions.

In 1989 a pair of peregrine falcons appeared, soaring near the cliffs over Jordan Pond. The sight encouraged park biologists, who had spent the last few years working with College of the Atlantic professor William Drury and a national program to reintroduce the birds after the ban on DDT. They created a plan to bring peregrines back to Acadia in a process called "hacking." A Coast Guard helicopter and five men transported the necessary equipment to Jordan Cliffs. Seven chicks raised at Cornell University's Ornithology Lab were delivered to Acadia and placed in a wooden box to simulate a nest, in the hopes that the young birds would imprint the site upon their memory. Stewards camped nearby to monitor the birds and dropped food onto the ledge from above. They repeated the process for several years, with adults sighted in 1989 and 1990.

In 1991 a pair of falcons arrived at the Precipice Cliffs on the eastern side of Champlain Mountain. By June they had established a territory and, for the first time in nearly forty years, falcon chicks born at Acadia fledged, flying away from the granite ledges into the world. Barbara Patterson, who surely rejoiced at these efforts, died later the same year.

The return of peregrine falcons bolstered morale among resource managers. The partnership with universities and organizations also demonstrated that to truly restore and protect the resources, to be the stewards that Judy Hazen Connery wanted to be, Acadia's natural resource managers had to work with others.

The US Department of Agriculture mapped soils. The Maine Department of Inland Fisheries and Wildlife helped protect eagle nesting habitat. Earthwatch volunteers documented plants and animals of the smaller islands alongside park staff, many of whom had never before been to the islands. The Nature Conservancy, US Geological Survey, and Maine Department of Conservation helped map vegetation. Friends of Acadia and others prevented the clear-cutting of Schoodic's forests.

Conservation, too, required partnership beyond the political boundary of the park.

Back in 1933, the Fauna of the National Parks survey team repeatedly emphasized the need for parks to protect habitat for migrating wildlife. The designated boundaries of Acadia and other early national

Peregrine falcon chicks at the Precipice. ACADIA NATIONAL PARK

parks did not account for annual migration patterns; the parks were like houses "with two sides left open." It was impossible for parks to protect animals when they only lived in the park for part of the year.

Aided by new technologies, such as digital mapping, and the development of landscape ecology science that viewed land as a mosaic of patches, corridors, and stepping stones, the Acadia vision grew.

What had started on Mount Desert Island as a movement to protect beautiful places, and the experience of walking through them, became part of a larger landscape conservation effort. The National Park Service,

US Fish and Wildlife Service, Maine Coast Heritage Trust, Frenchman Bay Conservancy, and other public and private interests came together to envision a network of protected lands and islands from Isle au Haut to Schoodic Point and beyond.

Their motivations were the same as those of Eliza Homans, George Dorr, and John D. Rockefeller Jr.: to protect plants and animals, ensure clean water, create opportunities for recreation and public access. Perhaps most of all, at the end of their lives, people wanted to sail away from Mount Desert Island, through the spruce and bedrock islands and the cries of falcons and gulls, into the fog, knowing they had given back to a place that had given them so much. Their greatest motivation was love.

Buckle Island. A. HOPKINS

In April 1971, Peggy Rockefeller donated a conservation easement on Buckle Island to Acadia National Park. There was an old cabin on the island, a small structure the Rockefellers built to teach their children the value of self-reliance. David Rockefeller cleared the trails, and the family would spend a night or two on the island when they could. Peggy felt that "the handmade life and the life of the imagination were, in combination with nature, the greatest teachers of fundamental values," daughter Eileen Rockefeller said in an interview with the *New York Times*. "It was a powerful place."

In the decades since the Rockefellers donated the conservation easement, the cabin fell apart. But, as in so many other parts of Acadia, the wild never fully eclipses the evidence of human hands.

At the end of a narrow path through the dark spruce forest of Buckle Island, a green door hangs from a crude frame between two trees. The door opens to the other side of the forest. Lit by the rays of the sun setting into the ocean, another day ends on the wilderness of Acadia, where an open door can always be found.

BIBLIOGRAPHY

Abbe Museum. 2015. Permanent exhibit. Bar Harbor, ME.

Agassiz, L. 1867. "Glacial Phenomena in Maine." *Atlantic Monthly* 19 (February): 211–18; (March): 286.

Allaback, S. 2000. *Mission 66 Visitor Centers: The History of a Building Type*. Washington, DC: National Park Service.

Anonymous. 1866. *The Cruise of the Forest Home, or Chronicles of A Pleasure Trip to Mount Desert*. New York: Francis Hart and Company.

Anonymous. 1872. "Mount Desert." *Harper's New Monthly Magazine* 45: 321–341.

Anonymous. 1929. "Bar Harbor and Acadia National Park Park, Maine: A Scenic Wonderland of Ocean, Lakes and Mountains." Bar Harbor: Sherman Publishing Company.

Appalachian Mountain Club Bulletin XVI. "Echo Lake Camp." (April 1923): 125–126.

Arflack, C., C. Schmitt, and A. J. Miller-Rushing. 2012. "History of botanical exploration and collecting on Mount Desert Island and in Acadia National Park, Maine," unpublished manuscript, Acadia National Park.

Baldwin, L. S. 2008. *Asticou Azalea Garden: The Work of Charles K. Savage*. Seal Harbor, ME: Mount Desert Land & Garden Preserve.

———. 2008. *Thuya Garden: Asticou Terraces & Thuya Lodge*. Seal Harbor, ME: Mount Desert Land & Garden Preserve.

Barter, C. S., M. C. Brown, J. T. Stakely, and G. J. Stellpflug. 2006. *Acadia Trails Treatment Plan, Cultural Landscape Report for the Historical Trail System of Acadia National Park, Maine*. Boston: Olmsted Center for Landscape Preservation and National Park Service.

Barton, A. M., A. S. White, and C. V. Cogbill. 2012. *The Changing Nature of the Maine Woods*. Durham: University of New Hampshire Press.

Bates, A. 1885. "Isle au Haut." *Outing* 6: 649–56. Boston: Wheelman Company.

Beatrix Farrand Society. www.beatrixfarrandsociety.org.

Bedell, R. 2001. *The Anatomy of Nature: Geology and American Landscape Painting, 1825–1875*. Princeton, NJ: Princeton University Press.

Belanger, P. J. 1999. *Inventing Acadia: Artists and Tourists at Mount Desert*. Rockland, ME: Farnsworth Art Museum.

Biggar, H. P. 1922. *The Works of Samuel de Champlain: Volume I, 1599–1607*. Toronto: Champlain Society.

Bishop, W. H. 1885. "Fish and men in the Maine islands." *Harper's* Handy Series 15: July 24, 1885. New York: Harper and Brothers.

Bond, J. 1967. *Native Birds of Mount Desert Island.* Philadelphia: The Academy of Natural Sciences of Philadelphia.

Borns, H. W. Jr., and K. A. Maasch. 2015. *Foot Steps of the Ancient Great Glacier of North America.* Switzerland: Springer.

Brown, J. 1995. *Beatrix: The Gardening Life of Beatrix Jones Farrand, 1872–1959.* New York: Viking.

Brown, M. C. 2006. *Pathmakers: Cultural Landscape Report for the Historical Trail System of Acadia National Park, Maine.* Boston: Olmsted Center for Landscape Preservation and National Park Service.

Bryant, W. C. 1872. *Picturesque America; or, the Land We Live In.* New York: D. Appleton and Company.

Carter, R. 1864. *A Summer Cruise on the Coast of New England.* Boston: Crosby and Nichols.

The Champlain Society. The Champlain Society Collection. Mount Desert, ME: Mount Desert Island Historical Society.

Chasse, P. 2004. "Beatrix Farrand (1872–1959)." *Chebacco* 6: 64–69.

Chernow, R. 1998. *Titan: The Life of John D. Rockefeller, Sr.* New York: Random House.

[Church, F. E.] 1850. "Mountain views and coast scenery, by a landscape painter." *Bulletin of the American Art-Union.* November 1850: 130–131.

Clark, J., and G. Neptune. 2014. "The Wabanaki and the Mount Desert Island Region before Colonization." *Friends of Acadia Journal,* Spring.

Cole, T. 1836. "Essay on American Scenery." *American Monthly* 1:1–12.

Committee on the Public Lands. 1918. "Hearing before the Subcommittee of the Committee on the Public Lands, House of Representatives, 65th Congress 2nd Session on H.R. 11935, A Bill to Establish the Mount Desert National Park in the State of Maine, May 30, 1918." Washington, DC: Government Printing Office.

DeCosta, B. F. 1868. *Scenes in the Isle of Mount Desert, Coast of Maine.* New York.

Deur, D. 2013. *The Park Lands of Isle au Haut: A Community Oral History.* Boston: National Park Service.

Dorr, G. B. 1929. "Acadia National Park: A Seacoast Possession of the Nation." *Nature Magazine* 13 (5): 315–19.

———. 1942. *Acadia National Park, Its Origin and Background.* Bangor, ME: Burr Printing.

———. 1985. *The Story of Acadia National Park.* Bar Harbor, ME: Acadia Publishing.

Dorr, G. B., M. L. Fernald, and E. N. Forbush. 1914. "The Unique Island of Mount Desert." *National Geographic* 26: 75–89.

Drake, S. A. 1875. *Nooks and Corners of the New England Coast.* New York: Harper.

Eckstorm, F. J. 1932. *Handicrafts of the Modern Indians of Maine, Bulletin III.* Bar Harbor, ME: Abbe Museum, Lafayette National Park.

Eliot, C. Charles Eliot papers. Loeb Library Archives, Harvard University.

———. 1890. "The coast of Maine." *Garden and Forest.* February 19: 86–87.

Eliot, C. W. 1904. *The Right Development of Mount Desert*. Privately printed.
———. 1914. "The Need of Conserving the Beauty and Freedom of Nature in Modern Life." *National Geographic* 26: 67–75.
Eliot, C. W. II. 1928. "The Future of Mount Desert Island: A Report to the Plan Committee of Bar Harbor Village Improvement Association." Bar Harbor, ME: Bar Harbor Village Improvement Association.
Eliot, S. A. 1939. "A Brief Record of the Origin and Activities of the Hancock County Trustees of Public Reservations," pp. 7–14 in *The Hancock County Trustees of Public Reservations: An Historical Sketch and a Record of the Holdings of the Trustees*. Bar Harbor, ME.
Epp, R. 2014. "The Bowl, the Beehive, and a Secular Epiphany." *Friends of Acadia Journal*, Winter.
Farrand, B. 1946. "The Start and the Goal." *Reef Point Gardens Bulletin* 1 (1): 1–4.
Foulds, H. E., and L. G. Meier. 1993. "Historic Motor Road System, Acadia National Park, Compliance Documentation and Rehabilitation Guidelines for FHWA Project #PRA-ACAD-4A10." Cultural Landscape Publication No. 9. Boston: Olmsted Center for Landscape Preservation and National Park Service.
Gilman, R. A., C. A. Chapman, T. V. Lowell, and H. W. Borns Jr. 2011. *The Geology of Mount Desert Island: A Visitor's Guide to the Geology of Acadia National Park*. Augusta, ME.
Goldstein, J. S. 2014. *Majestic Mount Desert II*. Mount Desert, ME: Somes Pond Press.
Graham, J. 2010. "Acadia National Park: Geologic Resources Inventory Report." Natural Resources Report NPS/NRPC/GRD/NRR—2010/232. Fort Collins, CO: National Park Service.
Granston, D. W. III. 2013. "Getting Here from There: Steamboat Travel to Mount Desert Island." *Chebacco* 14: 19–36.
Hale, R. W. 1949. *The Story of Bar Harbor*. New York: Ives Washburn.
Heidenreich, C. E. 1976. "Explorations and Mapping of Samuel de Champlain, 1603–1632." Monograph No. 17, Supplement No. 2 to *Canadian Cartographer* Vol. 13. Toronto: University of Toronto Press.
Horner, B. 2013. "From Horses to Horsepower: Mount Desert Island's Ten-Year War for the Automobile." *Chebacco* 14: 86–106.
Hornsby, S. J., K. R. Sebold, P. Morrison, D. Sanger, and A. Faulkner. 1999. *Cultural Land Use Survey of Acadia National Park*. Orono: University of Maine.
Jackson, C. T. 1837. *First Report on the Geology of the State of Maine*. Augusta, ME: Smith and Robinson.
Jacobson, B., and H. Dominie. 1988. *Evaluation of Island Resources: Hancock County and Portion of Knox County, Maine*. Bar Harbor, ME: National Park Service.
Kandoian, N. A. 1994. "'Supreme and Distinctive' on the East Coast: The Mapping of Acadia National Park," pp. 2–46 in *Exploration and Mapping of the National Parks*, edited by J. M. Johnson. Winnetka, IL: Speculum Orbis Press.
Keefe, J., and S. Bushey. 2013. *Acadia National Park Waterproof Trail Map*, 3rd ed. Portland, ME: Map Adventures.
Land and Garden Preserve of Mount Desert Island, Maine. http://gardenpreserve.org.

Lane, F. K. 1922. *The Letters of Franklin K. Lane, personal and political*, edited by A. W. Lane and L. H. Wall. Boston and New York: Houghton Mifflin Company.

Lapham, W. B. 1886. *Bar Harbor and Mount Desert Island*. New York: Press of Liberty Printing Company.

Martin, C. B. 1867. *Mount Desert, on the Coast of Maine*. Portland, ME: B. Thurston and Company.

———. 1874. *Mount Desert, on the Coast of Maine*. Portland, ME: Loring, Short & Harmon.

McBride, B., and H. E. L. Prins. 2009. *Indians in Eden: Wabanakis & Rusticators on Maine's Mount Desert Island 1840s–1920s*. Camden, ME: Down East Books.

Minner, B. E. 2013. "The Bar Harbor Express: A Most Elegant Travel Option." *Chebacco* 14: 7–18.

Mittelhauser, G. H., L. L. Gregory, S. C. Rooney, and J. E. Weber. 2010. *The Plants of Acadia National Park*. Orono: University of Maine Press.

Molen van Ee, P. "Maps of Acadia National Park." Mapping the National Parks, Library of Congress. www.loc.gov/collection/national-parks-maps/articles-and -essays/maps-of-acadia-national-park.

Moore, B. 1921. "Scientific Aspects of Mt. Desert Island." *Maine Naturalist* 1 (2): 100–101.

Moore, B., and N. Taylor. 1927. *Vegetation of Mount Desert Island, Maine, and its Environment. Brooklyn Botanic Garden Memoirs*, vol. 3.

Moreira, J., P. Dean, A. Dudley, and K. Champney. 2009. *The Civilian Conservation Corps at Acadia National Park*. Bar Harbor, ME: National Park Service.

Morrison, P. 2005. *History of the Bar Harbor Water Company*, prepared for the National Park Service. Bar Harbor, ME: Crane & Morrison Archaeology and Abbe Museum.

Mount Desert Island Community Heritage Project, in partnership with Maine Memory Network. *Mount Desert Island: Shaped by Nature*. http://mdi.mainememory .net/page/3646/display.html.

National Oceanic and Atmospheric Administration, Office of Coast Survey. Historical Map & Chart Collection. http://historicalcharts.noaa.gov.

———, US Coast and Geodetic Survey Annual Reports. www.lib.noaa.gov/collections/ imgdocmaps/cgs_annual_reports.html.

National Park Service. 1992. "General Management Plan, Acadia National Park, Maine." US Department of the Interior.

———. 2002. "Hiking Trails Management Plan, Acadia National Park, Maine." NPS D-254. US Department of the Interior.

———. 2015. Acadia National Park Annual Visitation, 1904–2014. Bar Harbor, ME.

———. 2015. Acadia National Park, Fire of 1947. www.nps.gov/acad/historyculture/ fireof1947.htm.

———. 2015. Acadia National Park, Vegetation Program. www.nps.gov/acad/parkmgmt/ rm_vegetation.htm.

Neptune, G. 2015. "Naming the Dawnland: Wabanaki Place Names." *Chebacco* 16: 92–108.

Patterson, W. A., K. E. Saunders, and L. J. Horton. 1983. "Fire Regimes of the Coastal Maine Forests of Acadia National Park," OSS 83-3. National Park Service.

Peabody, H., and C. H. Grandgent. 1928. *Walks on Mount Desert Island, Maine.* Boston: H. Peabody.

Prins, H. E. L., and B. McBride. 2007. *Asticou's Island Domain: Wabanakis at Mount Desert Island 1500–2000.* Acadia National Park Ethnographic Overview & Assessment. Boston: National Park Service.

Rand, E. L. 1889. "The Woods of Mount Desert Island." *Garden and Forest.* October 9, 483–84.

Rand, E. L., and J. H. Redfield. 1894. *Flora of Mount Desert Island, Maine.* Cambridge, MA: John Wilson and Son.

Ristow, W. W. 1985. *American Maps and Mapmakers.* Detroit: Wayne State University Press.

Robert Abbe Museum. 1978. *The First Fifty Years of the Robert Abbe Museum of Stone Age Antiquities and a Look Ahead, August 14, 1928–August 14, 1978.* Bulletin 11. Bar Harbor, ME: Courier-Gazette.

Roberts, A. R. 1990. *Mr. Rockefeller's Roads: The Untold Story of Acadia's Carriage Roads & Their Creator.* Camden, ME: Down East.

Savage, A. C. (unpublished manuscript). "Memories of a Lifetime." Northeast Harbor, ME: Northeast Harbor Library.

Schauffler, M., and G. L. Jacobson, Jr. 2002. "Persistence of Coastal Spruce Refugia during the Holocene in Northern New England, USA, Detected by Stand-Scale Pollen Stratigraphies." *Journal of Ecology* 90: 235–50.

Sellars, R. W. 1997. *Preserving Nature in the National Parks: A History.* New Haven, CT: Yale University Press.

Shaler, N. S. 1874. "Recent Changes of Level on the Coast of Maine." *Memoirs of the Boston Society of Natural History* 2: 321–40.

———. 1889. "Geology of Mount Desert," pp. 993–1,061 in *Eighth Annual Report of the U.S. Geological Survey to the Secretary of the Interior, 1886–1887, Part II.* Washington, DC: Government Printing Office.

———. 1909. *The Autobiography of Nathaniel Southgate Shaler.* Boston: Houghton Mifflin.

Shettleworth, E. 2015. *The History of Maine Photography.* Camden, ME: Down East.

Shinn, C. H. 1884. "From Mission Peak to Mount Desert." *The Overland Monthly* 5 (October): 427–33.

Smith, D. C., and H. W. Borns. 2000. "Louis Agassiz, the Great Deluge, and Early Maine Geology." *Northeastern Naturalist* 7: 157–77.

Smythe, C. W. 2008. *Traditional Uses of Fish Houses in Otter Cove.* Bar Harbor, ME: National Park Service.

———. 1926. "Echo Lake Camp." *Appalachia* 16 (1926) 367.

Street, G. E. 1905. *Mount Desert: A History.* Boston: Houghton Mifflin Company.

Sweetser, M. F. 1883. *Summer Days Down East.* Portland, ME: Chisholm Brothers.

Tankard, J. 2009. *Beatrix Farrand: Private Gardens, Public Landscapes.* New York: Monacelli Press.

Tracy, C. 1997. *The Tracy Logbook, 1855.* Bar Harbor, ME: Acadia Publishing Co.

Wherry, E. T. 1928. *Wild Flowers of Mount Desert Island, Maine.* Bar Harbor: Garden Club of Mount Desert.

Wilmerding, J. 1994. *The Artist's Mount Desert: American Painters on the Maine Coast.* Princeton, NJ: Princeton University Press.

———. 2012. *Maine Sublime: Frederic Edwin Church's Landscapes of Mount Desert and Mount Katahdin.* Hudson, NY: Olana Partnership.

Winthrop, J. 1630. *Original Narratives of Early American History: Winthrop's Journal 1630–1649 Volume I.* (J. K. Hosmer, editor). New York: Scribner.

Workman, A. K. 2014. *Schoodic Point: History on the Edge of Acadia National Park.* Charleston, SC: History Press.

Yard, R. S. 1916. "The Business of Scenery." *The Nation's Business* 4 (6): 10–11.

INDEX

About the Author

Catherine Schmitt is the author of *The President's Salmon: Restoring the King of Fish and its Home Waters* and *A Coastal Companion: A Year in the Gulf of Maine from Cape Cod to Canada*. Her writing is informed by her scientific background, which includes experience studying lakes, streams, wetlands, and beaches throughout the Northeast. She directs communications for the Maine Sea Grant College Program at the University of Maine, where she also teaches science writing and composition. Visit catherineschmitt.com for an archive of published work and book-related events.